GOLDEN

OPPORTUNITY

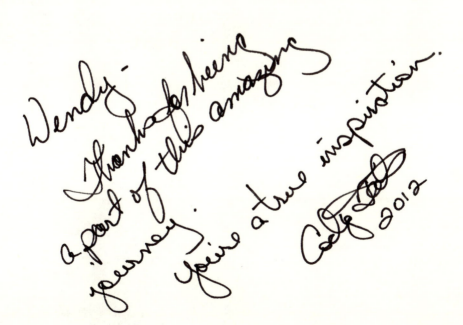

Wendy –
Thank you for being
a part of this amazing
journey.
You're a true inspiration.

2012

GOLDEN
OPPORTUNITY

REMARKABLE CAREERS
THAT BEGAN AT
McDONALD'S

CODY TEETS

CIDER MILL
PRESS

BOOK
PUBLISHERS

13-Digit ISBN: 978-1-60433-279-7
10-Digit ISBN: 1-60433-279-4

Please support your local bookseller first!

Books published by Cider Mill Press Book Publishers are available at
special discounts for bulk purchases in the United States by corporations,
institutions, and other organizations. For more information, please contact
the publisher.

Cider Mill Press Book Publishers
"Where good books are ready for press"
12 Port Farm Road
Kennebunkport, Maine 04046

Visit us on the web!
www.cidermillpress.com

Editorial and production services provided by
Winans Kuenstler Publishing, LLC
Cover design by Whitney Cookman
Printed in the United States

1 2 3 4 5 6 7 8 9 0
First Edition

To my husband, Dan—
  from high school through college,
  from relocations to babies,
  from tired days to great days,
  thanks for standing by me. I love you.
To my mom, Roseann—
  thanks for creating the environment where
  we didn't know what we did not have.
  Your strength and guidance on my journey
  made me who I am. I love you.

CONTENTS

Acknowledgments

"If you want to lift yourself up, lift up someone else."
—Booker T. Washington

When I think about the many individuals to appreciate and thank, I am reminded of the African proverb, "It takes a village." The proverb teaches that for an individual to be productive and well-rounded they need not just strong family values but a solid community. Eventually, we all interact with people other than our relatives.

In putting this book together, I have had the opportunity to spend many hours over several years learning and growing with the assistance of those who have cared enough to take an interest. While there are too many to mention here, I have a strong belief that people come into our lives for a reason. Through these associations, I have had the opportunity to learn from you, my friends, coworkers, franchisees, and family members.

To Gina Otto—thanks for your friendship and inspiration. A spark of an idea can light up the world.

To Colton and Jackson—my two boys. Being your mom is God's greatest gift.

To my family—you know me the best and love me the most. Thanks for being with me through the ups and downs. I love you all very much.

To Cody Robertson—you have been a strong role model to me and many others.

To Bob Charles—thanks for opening the door that allowed me to fly.

To my Rocky Mountain McDonald's Team—you are a first-class group of professionals who know how to make a plan a reality. Judi Martshenko and Jim Bath—thanks for ensuring I keep all the balls in the air.

To Foster Winans—thanks for organizing my thoughts and sharing my vision in a creative manner.

Thanks to my many mentors, coaches, and thought partners who had the courage and caring to provide me with feedback, guidance, and wisdom. Never underestimate your impact and contributions to the achievement of a dream. In alphabetical order: L. Adams, L. Anderson, Arlt Family, D. Armstrong, Asfaw Family, T. Belisle, J. Betz, M. Bullington, J. Burroughs, M. Boyles, Brownstein Family, D. Coughlin, J. Campbell, T. Carlson, K. Cinocco, K. Clement, C. Cole, R. Colon, C. Cook, R. Ellis, J. Fields, S. Finn, C. Freitag, E. Gallender, D. Haley, N. Golden, A. Gomez, M. Hadwin, D. Hamilton, M. Havenga, Heriaud Family, J. Hopewell, C. Hunter, K. Hoyman, M. Kanjee, J. Johnson, F. Jones, Jones Family, M. Jurineack, R. Kennan, C. Kramer, R. Layton, Lewis Family, O. Melendrez-Kumph, S. Manning, J. Marcos, M. Mayer, McAvoy Family, S. McCullough, A. Mestas, D. Morris, E. Navarro, L. Nelson, K. Newell, R. Nibeel, J. Norberg, J. Olson, B. O'Rourke, R. Parrish, S. Peterson, S. Plotkin, S. Ramirez, S. Rogers-Reece, M. Roberts, Sandoval Family, M. Seaman, A. Seecharan, J. Smith, B. Selle, J. Stratton, Sparrer Family, B. Steinhilper, Stingley Family, B. Stringfellow, D. Stockdale, Suer Family, D. Thompson, B. Unger, R. Valdez, I. Villasenor, F. Vizcarra, K. Voetberg, A. Watson, Webb Family, B. Whitman, J. Weidemann, P. Widdicombe, Zamora Family.

To all those who agreed to be interviewed for this book and took time to share their stories—thanks for helping me spread the word that entry-level work is more than a McJob, and never a dead end.

To Bill Garrett—I have been honored to work alongside you for the past five years.

"For I know the plans I have for you," said the Lord. "They are plans for good and not disaster, to give you a future and a hope."

Jeremiah 29:11

Foreword

Not long after my association with McDonald's began in 1963 in Washington, DC—when I became the first Ronald McDonald—I walked into one of the restaurants in the area and spotted a friend working behind the counter, wearing the same signature paper hat as the kids working on crew. He had been a top executive at Marriott. I had heard he was changing jobs, but I had imagined something a bit grander than manning the register at a McDonald's.

"What are you doing here?" I asked. The place was humming with customers and kids frying, grilling, assembling orders, pouring drinks, and cleaning up. In between greeting customers and delivering meals, he explained that he'd accepted an executive post with McDonald's. "They like all their people to learn how to work behind the counter before they settle in. It's part of the orientation."

I was impressed. Here was a guy who had earned his stripes in the corporate suite and was moving up the ladder, yet the company recognized the value of its leaders learning what was happening on the front lines. I remembered the incident when I spoke with Cody Teets about this book about people who started out on those front lines and ended up becoming accomplished in various fields.

Unlike the people you'll meet in these pages, my career was well under way when I was hired by McDonald's. I had hosted a popular kids' show on local TV. I played Bozo the Clown, a character with a huge following played by many different people in different markets around the country. McDonald's advertised on the show, and I had made some appearances as Bozo at McDonald's that drew big crowds. I loved clowning in the restaurants because it was fun to make all those kids laugh. We had as many as 5,000 people show up at some of those appearances.

Bozo went off the air in 1962, but I had a chance to continue clowning when the local McDonald's franchisee asked its ad agency to come up with a replacement character they could use in their television commercials and local events. An ex-Bozo fit the bill.

When it came time to create the costume and name the character, I suggested Donald McDonald, but the folks at the agency liked the sound of Ronald better. My concept was simple—I remember writing it on a scrap of paper: *Ronald likes to do everything kids like to do. He's a big clown, but he likes to play on swings, run around, swim, roller-skate, and so on.* That was the key to the character's success—he was a big kid.

Thus was born a name and an iconic figure who today is nearly as revered and recognized as Santa among American kids. He also became the inspiration for what has become a worldwide network of more than three hundred Ronald McDonald Houses providing lodging and other support services to more than three million families of sick children each year.

I can't say that being the first Ronald McDonald launched my career because when Ronald went national in 1963, I retired my costume and later moved on to television, first as a local weatherman in Washington and in 1980 joining NBC's *Today Show.* I *can* say that I took the job of clowning seriously and, as many of the people in this book learned to do in their first jobs, paid attention to every detail. In my case that meant staying true to the gentle, caring nature of the character, and always giving it my best.

Occasionally the experience was profound, like the time I got a call from The Children's Hospital of Washington that a little girl dying of leukemia had asked her mother and father if she could meet Ronald. I had my costume when the call came, so I was able to go right over. Her face lit up when I entered the room, and she got a big kick out of my antics. She was very sick, so I only stayed a couple of minutes. As I left, I bent down and kissed her on the forehead. Her parents thanked me. Three days later, she died and I was glad I'd listened to my instinct telling me to go when I did.

Even small gestures can leave a big impression, a foundation on which McDonald's founder Ray Kroc built an empire. I was reminded of that ten years ago when a cab driver recognized me and, to my astonishment, recalled an encounter that had taken place some thirty years prior.

"I met you once before," he said, eyeing me in the rearview mirror.

"Oh, really? Where did we meet?"

"At McDonald's in Anacostia." That was an inner-city neighborhood of Washington, the site of many of the hundreds of events I did. The kids lined up out the door just to get a chance to meet Ronald, shake his hand, and giggle when he honked his hidden horn.

"Yeah, my little boy's shoe was untied," the driver said. "You noticed his shoe was untied, and you reached down and tied his laces for him. I never forgot that."

The stories in this book are rich with moments like these that people recall from their first jobs when they were teens and young adults, experiences that helped shape their self-images, work habits, attitudes, skills, and ambitions. I like to think the course of my career and the impressions I've left are evidence that there's no such thing as "just a clown." The people you'll meet here are similarly living proof that there's no such thing as "just a McJob."

—Willard H. Scott

Introduction

C hances are good that someone you know has worked at a McDonald's restaurant. In the decades since the company's founding in 1955, it's estimated that one in ten Americans— about 20 million people—have at some point or another pinned a McDonald's name tag on their uniforms. Each year, the company and its franchisees employ more than 800,000 people. The majority are teenagers and young adults for whom the experience is a landmark rite of passage. It's when they receive their first real paychecks, when they have their first taste of independence, and where they learn their first real-world lessons about being on time, arriving prepared, working as a team, taking responsibility, and performing under pressure.

My McDonald's rite of passage began in October 1980 when I became one of those teenagers. One of the defining moments was when I came home from my new job at a restaurant in the Denver area to proudly show my mother the first paycheck I earned under the Golden Arches. During the thirty years since, I've been proud of all the McDonald's paychecks I've earned as I moved up the ladder to my current position as one of two dozen regional vice presidents and general manager of the 780-restaurant Rocky Mountain region.

Along the way I've had to grin and bear all the disparaging comments about flipping burgers and "Fries with that?" I've endured the derogatory portrayals of quick-serve restaurant workers in films and on television and the addition to dictionaries of the word *McJob*, defined by the *Merriam-Webster Unabridged* as "a low-paying job that requires little skill and provides little opportunity for advancement."

When I started working at McDonald's at age sixteen I assumed, like millions of others have, that I would work there until I was ready to start my real career, which I thought might be in marketing. Not only did my "McJob" turn out to be anything but a dead end, it also launched me on a journey that has been fun, personally rewarding, and allowed me to achieve a degree of financial security that made it possible for me to pay it forward, including donating the profits from this book to Ronald McDonald House Children's Charities.

My story is the rule rather than the exception to the McJob myth, which inaccurately denigrates much of the quick-service restaurant industry and other sectors like retail and convenience stores. You know things have gotten mixed up when it's said to be "just a McJob" to work at a McDonald's, but working at a Starbucks for about the same pay earns the hip title "barista."

As of this writing, former crew members like myself make up more than 70 percent of McDonald's restaurant managers (who can earn more than $50,000 a year plus a bonus and a company car), more than half of McDonald's franchisees (whose restaurants average annual revenues of more than $2 million), and more than 30 percent of McDonald's executives, including our most recent CEO Jim Skinner and McDonald's USA president Jan Fields.

Educators and public officials who speak of the importance of making sure our kids can get a college degree "so they don't end up flipping burgers" may mean well, but they are perpetuating an idea unsupported by the facts. As author Charles J. Sykes wrote in his 2007 book *50 Rules Kids Won't Learn In School*, "Your grandparents had a different word for burger flipping. They called it 'opportunity.'"

Contemplating the bad rap that working at McDonald's had gotten, I began to wonder a few years ago how the experience shaped the careers of so many millions of others, including those who moved on. I wondered how working on crew might have informed their outlooks on life, taught them valuable skills, and affected their attitudes about work. That curiosity was the inspiration for this book.

I began collecting stories of people who started at McDonald's and went on to create remarkable and rewarding careers, both within the McDonald's family and in other fields. Several themes emerged early on. Many people said they learned discipline, gained self-confidence, and came away with a model for leadership and teamwork that has helped them throughout their working lives. A majority came from modest backgrounds, as I did, and some were new Americans—immigrants—who left their native countries and cultures behind to strive for the American dream.

Alma Anguiano, a McDonald's human resources executive, crossed the border from Mexico as an infant, grew up in a rough neighborhood of Los Angeles, became the first English-speaker in her family, and was the first to earn a college degree while working at a McDonald's restaurant.

Kyong Kapalczynski was born in South Korea, married an American soldier, and arrived in the US speaking no English. She was determined to work at a McDonald's because she loved the cheeseburgers. When she got her first job on crew, she endured teasing because of her accent and rudimentary vocabulary and was made to do more than her share of bathroom-cleaning duty. Today she owns four restaurants in Montana.

Ed Sanchez came from Cuba with his mother in the 1960s with only the clothes on their backs. He began his career at sixteen at a McDonald's in Miami cleaning tables in the lobby. Today he is chairman of Lopez Foods, a supplier of meat products to McDonald's.

The stories you'll find in these pages are all inspirational in one way or another. Jay Leno credits a McDonald's owner/operator for encouraging him to enter a company talent show that proved to be the spark for his career as a comedian and entertainer. Former White House Chief of Staff Andrew H. Card, Jr., worked his way through college at a McDonald's, honing the leadership skills that he credits with preparing him for his many roles in government. Astronaut Leroy Chiao worked in a McDonald's in California where he learned the skill of interacting with many different people doing many different jobs to accomplish a common goal, much like the NASA missions which he would later fly.

What I've learned from all of these people, and what I hope to convey by assembling their stories in one place, is that there's no such thing as a dead-end job. A job may be hard, risky, low-paying, unchallenging, or inconvenient. But every job offers a person who wants to learn a chance to grow, even if it's only by discovering what he or she dislikes.

So long as people give it their all, act in good faith, and are paid an honest dollar for an honest day's work, every job, no matter how mundane, can be as noble as the highest paying or the most influential. For impressionable teenagers in particular, their first jobs establish attitudes about work and responsibility that they carry into adulthood.

It's also my hope that the accumulated evidence debunking the McJob myth may help parents come to understand that working at McDonald's is no obstacle to the social mobility of their children. In the process of collecting these stories, I've heard that parents of college students are often reluctant to let their children work in a quick-service restaurant like McDonald's because they don't know how to explain to family and friends why their kids "can't do any better."

Once again, the facts undermine the myth. I got my college degree *while* flipping burgers. So have hundreds of thousands of others over the past half century. Thousands of people earned their first college credits, and in some cases their associate degrees, at Hamburger University. The company's accredited school offers classes in accounting and marketing as well as restaurant management.

By the time I was in college I had received several promotions at McDonald's and realized that I could make more money staying where I was than at an entry-level marketing job. To leave would have meant starting over in a new field without a clear path to success.

Because of its practice of hiring from within, to stay at McDonald's allowed me to follow a well-lit path. I had acquired a circle of trusted coworkers and supervisors whose mission was to help me reach my goals. Nowhere could I see a sign that said Dead End. I made a conscious choice to see where the path would lead and haven't looked back since.

Parents who worry that their kids risk falling short of their potential by choosing to work in a quick-service restaurant are missing the value of self-respect that young people get from work. Many teens and young adults enjoy the fast pace of a restaurant and having a chance to explore their abilities. They enjoy working with other young people in a collaborative enterprise, meeting and serving the wide variety of people who come through the doors or the drive-thrus, and most especially earning their own spending money.

Parents play a big role in setting expectations for their sons and daughters. No one understands this idea better than Andrew Card, who said he and his wife insisted that their oldest daughter take a job in a quick-service restaurant when she turned sixteen. She did, donning a cowboy hat at a Roy Rogers.

"Did she need the money?" Card said. "Probably not. Did she need to learn how to work? Absolutely."

There's a bigger picture here as well. In the wake of the Great Recession we hear about America losing its glow as the land of opportunity. Stubbornly high unemployment among eighteen- to twenty-five-year-olds has led to predictions that an entire generation may face permanent underemployment. Yet in the midst of the worst economy since the Great Depression, McDonald's and its franchisees struggle at times to fill positions. Each year they need to hire roughly 400,000 new employees to replace the young people who are going off to college or to start careers in other professions.

One of the more insidious misconceptions dispelled by the stories in this book is that quick-service restaurant jobs are by definition unskilled labor. The truth is that young people who go to work at McDonald's receive intensive, supportive training from their first day. They quickly become skilled at customer service, food preparation and sanitation, and, as so many of the people in this book have said, how to work together.

In the first several years, promotions can come fast, and it's not uncommon for eighteen- and nineteen-year-olds to be training newcomers and managing entire shifts of up to a dozen workers. If there's another major enterprise where an eighteen-year-old has the chance to learn and be trusted with that much leadership responsibility, I have yet to hear of it.

The value of organizational and leadership skills is illustrated in the stories of people like Laurieann Gibson, a choreographer whose clients have included Lady Gaga. Laurieann said she has drawn on what she learned as a teenager working at McDonald's to build the collaborations required to design and produce her electrifying performances.

Mike Grice, a lieutenant in the United States Marine Corps, said McDonald's helped teach him how to manage stressful situations where many things need to happen at once. He told me that what he learned during the lunch rush served him well during his tour of duty in Afghanistan when his unit was deployed to interact with units from several coalition partners and the Afghan military.

Finally, the notion that working at a McDonald's holds little opportunity for advancement is betrayed by the fact that so many of the restaurant supervisors, managers, owner/operators, and vendors are minorities and immigrants who have achieved the American dream starting with a spatula in their hands.

Henry "Hank" Thomas, one of the original Freedom Riders of the civil rights movement, started out assembling hamburgers at a McDonald's in Washington, DC. In the years that followed, he and members of his family have owned eight McDonald's and are partners in three Marriott hotels.

Little skill? Little opportunity for advancement? Dead end? The many voices in this book tell a different story—colorful, inspiring, heartwarming, optimistic, and as American as hamburgers, milkshakes, and French fries.

The profiles are arranged chronologically based on when each person first worked in a McDonald's restaurant, beginning in 1955 with Lester Stein. Lester worked in the first McDonald's in Des Plaines, Illinois, with founder Ray Kroc occasionally looking over his shoulder and offering suggestions for how to do his job more efficiently.

The last profile is of Peruvian-born Fatima Poggi—now twenty years old—who immigrated to the US at age ten and got her first real job at a McDonald's in Michigan just four years ago. Much like Jay Leno's story, Fatima was encouraged by her owner/operator to enter a McDonald's talent contest, called Voice of McDonald's. The biannual *American Idol*-style competition drew more than 10,000 video entries from McDonald's employees around the world. By the time it was over, Fatima had performed live before a large audience and a panel of music industry judges. Today she is an up-and-coming recording artist with a growing Latino fan base and a bright future.

If you read from beginning to end, you will get a real sense of how the company and the country evolved since 1955. And I hope those who read these stories will rethink their prejudices and find potential where they now see underachievement.

What's particularly remarkable is that you can draw a straight line from the standards and culture that Lester Stein learned in Ray Kroc's first restaurant in 1955 to the values and practices that 400,000 new employees learn every year in more than 14,000 restaurants in the US alone.

However you choose to read this book—chronologically or just dropping in here and there—these are all quintessentially American stories that celebrate the adage that this country, more than any other on earth, is still a land of opportunity.

—*Cody R. Teets*
Denver, Colorado 2012

GOLDEN
OPPORTUNITY

*L*et us hope that whatever your future
you will make the most of your experience
with McDonald's today.

—Ray A. Kroc
An Introduction to McDonald's
employee handbook, 1962

1950s

HIRED 1955

Lester E. Stein, Jr.

AUTHOR'S NOTE

Lester Stein was one of the first hires a month or so after the opening of the first restaurant in the McDonald's System, Inc. (predecessor of today's McDonald's Corporation). A new franchise enterprise founded by Ray A. Kroc in Chicago, it was located at 400 North Lee Street in nearby Des Plaines, Illinois. The restaurant opened for business on April 15, 1955.

Nearly six decades later, the lessons he learned are the same ones being taught each year to hundreds of thousands of new McDonald's crew members. Lester's feeling like part of a team is a sentiment expressed by every one of the people interviewed for this book. It is remarkable how far the company has come from those early years, when only men could work in the restaurants. Today a majority of the workforce are women and minorities. Lester met his wife because of his job at McDonald's. In July 2012, McDonald's agreed to host the Steins' fiftieth wedding anniversary at the museum that now stands at the site of the original restaurant.

Great leaders know they're in the spotlight all the time and constantly act as role models.

*I*n 1955 I was a second-year engineering student at Iowa State in Ames. When I came home for summer break that year, I discovered that this revolutionary new restaurant selling fifteen-cent hamburgers had opened a half block from my parents' house in Des Plaines, Illinois, a northern suburb of Chicago.

The restaurant was so close I could walk to it by crossing through the unfenced backyards between Oak Street, where we lived, and where it was located on Lee Street. I applied, got hired, and worked there all that summer and periodically over the next two and a half years, until I was drafted into the army.

McDonald's didn't hire women then, so the crew was made up of high school guys, other college-age men like me, and a half dozen or so fellows in their twenties and thirties who were air force reservists out of O'Hare Air Reserve Station. It was a close-knit group of men who seemed to benefit from the leadership and discipline of these older fellows.

Each of us was assigned a particular job. There was a French fry specialist; a couple of guys who flipped the burgers; someone who tended to the milkshake machine; and two guys at the front windows who greeted the customers, took the orders, and made change. It was exciting to be part of this new approach to selling fast food. The price was one of the main attractions: a hamburger was fifteen cents, dramatically less than the fifty cents or so you'd pay anywhere else.

The training program involved a manager or assistant manager showing you your job and then observing you as you did it until he thought you were proficient enough to do it on your own. There was a sense of camaraderie among the fellows that was both encouraged and organic. We all pitched in to make things run smoothly. Managers also placed a great deal of emphasis on sanitation and spotlessness. Any time you were caught up with your tasks, you were expected to grab a towel, mop, or broom and clean the counter and the machines, scrub the floor, clean the bathroom, or wash the outside walls.

Our restaurant was one where potential franchisees came to observe and, once they'd signed up, to be trained, so it was always busy. We learned that a franchise cost about $20,000 in those days, more than my entire college education. We all recognized and discussed among ourselves that this was a huge opportunity to get in on the ground floor of something big, but there was no way I'd have been able to raise that much money. Sure enough, those early owner/operators became millionaires many times over.

Ray Kroc, the brains behind the enterprise, was closely involved in his restaurants and was a stickler for perfection. We all dreaded the times when Ray's Cadillac pulled into the parking lot. "Oh, God! Here comes Ray," someone would shout. We knew that whatever we were doing was going to be closely observed—the man did a lot of hovering, directing, and correcting. He looked over my shoulder and made suggestions about how I could do my job more efficiently with less waste. He didn't bawl anyone out or give them a hard time. He did it in a very cordial way, more like a father figure, but he was still intimidating.

1955

Steve Jobs was born.

One of my most memorable lessons I learned by watching Ray when he wasn't observing us. He'd disappear and all of a sudden I'd look out the window and there he was with a hose in his hand, spraying the spills and debris off the parking area. Later on, I'd spot him out there on his hands and knees with a putty knife, scraping the gum off the asphalt.

It was impressive that the number one guy in the company took personal responsibility for every detail. To attract customers, you couldn't have garbage lying around or dirty counters or floors. He was probably in the parking lot thinking, All these kids are watching me, and I hope they're learning something from it.

I *was* watching, and I *was* learning a lesson in leadership. Great leaders know they're in the spotlight all the time and constantly act as role models.

Looking back, I consider the experience part of my college education. The most important lesson I learned was teamwork. Letting others know they can depend on you builds a spirit of cooperation. If you are willing to help other people, they will be willing to help you.

In the years that followed—a stint in the army in Korea, twenty-four years with Montgomery Ward, and finally a career in real estate—with every new assignment or position, I reflected on my McDonald's experience where I worked with others in a brand-new adventure. If I got a promotion, I would think, Hey, this is kind of like a McDonald's experience. It's all brand new, but it's going to be fun. If I go into it with the same attitude I had then, it ought to be good.

The work experiences I had when I was young and working at McDonald's were foundational and, in my case, life changing in the biggest way possible. I met my wife, Joanne, because of my job. Our two families lived across the street from each other. To get to work, I would cut through her family's backyard. Almost every day that first summer I'd see Joanne sitting outside reading a book or sunning herself, and we'd exchange a neighborly greeting.

After a while I got the feeling something was going on because she would always magically appear when I was walking by. Thus a romance was born. After we became friends, she'd come over to McDonald's and I'd sneak an extra patty in her burger or make her a special milkshake. She'd bring over some strawberries or other fresh fruit and I'd add it to the mixer. I was always terrified that Ray would find out and I'd get fired. He didn't, and our romance blossomed into marriage. We thank McDonald's for a successful fifty-year run so far.

We still live only a mile from Ray Kroc's first restaurant.

DID YOU KNOW?

First day sales at Des Plaines store: $366.12. The menu featured 7 products: hamburger, cheeseburger, fries, milkshakes, soft drinks, coffee, and milk.

HIRED 1956

James McGovern

AUTHOR'S NOTE

Many people have written about Ray Kroc and their experiences working with him or in the company, but I've never heard a story like Jim McGovern's. Like Lester Stein, Jim worked in the first McDonald's System restaurant in Des Plaines. Lester started at age fifteen and had the unusual experience of learning the business directly from Ray. That's an impressionable time of life, which may explain the passion with which he talks today about the many interactions he had with Ray and what he learned from them. Two of the lessons that impacted him in his later career as a supervisor in the electrical industry are timeless yet challenging to implement: no detail is too small; and being honest with superiors when you find yourself in over your head is better than trying to fake your way through.

At fifteen, you're not really exposed to the world and dealing with people like Ray Kroc—I never had to please anybody like that before—you grow up quick.

*I*t was quite an event in our town when the first McDonald's opened. Friends who worked there urged me to apply. As soon as I turned fifteen and could get a work permit, I did. It was a month or two before the manager called with the good news. I worked part-time through high school, from 1956 to 1958. My average paycheck was about twenty dollars a week.

We saw a lot of Ray Kroc because he parked his Cadillac at the restaurant each morning and walked to the station to catch the train to his Chicago office. He came back at night carrying a handful of discarded McDonald's bags and cups that he'd found on sidewalks and in gutters. If there had been too much for him to pick up, he told us kids, "Go walk into town and pick up every piece of paper along the way, whether it's ours or not. People don't know the difference."

On the weekends, when it was busy, Ray rolled up the sleeves of his white dress shirt, and with his gold watch and ring on, he picked up trash and hosed away the milkshake spills and mustard stains in the parking lot. Even when the manager would tell us to go out and help, Ray stayed out there with us, spraying the tile walls and brushing them off. He didn't seem to care if we were out there helping or not and looked like he was enjoying himself. That left a huge impression on me: no one was too important to pitch in—not even the boss.

Ray was always there on the weekends, which was when I almost always worked, so I was with him a lot. He critiqued us every minute of every day. I was raised to respect my elders and never talk back, so I got along great with him. Even when I disagreed with what he said, which was rare, I kept my opinions to myself.

I vividly remember my first day. As I walked to the front of the restaurant, Ray stopped me and said, "Son, you've got to remember something. You are an actor, that is your stage out there, and your audience is sitting in all the cars."

Suddenly I had a case of stage fright. I was afraid to go out front, thinking all the people sitting in their cars were watching us through the glass. It was profound way of thinking about what we did, and it helped me understand that he wanted everything to look perfect because every detail mattered.

One day when making milkshakes, I discovered just how perfect he wanted us to look. Before Ray started McDonald's, he had sold Multimixer milkshake machines to restaurants. Those five-head mixers were sacred because he had obtained the exclusive right to sell them, but using them could be tricky. Juggling five churning milkshakes required good timing when taking the cups off while the blades were spinning down. If you didn't take them off just right, the shake would splatter on those clean white shirts we all wore. I was still getting used to the machine and got some shake on my shirt. Ray noticed and told me to go change my shirt. After that, I stuffed a towel in my collar like a lobster bib to catch the splatters.

He was always reminding us kids, "Go wash your hands," or telling the older boys, "Why didn't you shave today? You can't come in here looking like that." Sideburns were in with teenaged boys, but out at McDonald's.

1956
Cost of a first-class stamp:
$0.03

Being fifteen, you're not really exposed to the world, but once you're working in a place like McDonald's and dealing with people like Ray Kroc—I never had to please anybody like that before—you grow up quick. There were fellows hired with me who didn't last because they didn't like the discipline.

Ray's motto, which I've used all my life, was, "Many little leaks will sink the ship." People have questioned me during my career, "Why are you worrying about such stupid little things?" What Ray Kroc taught me is that a lot of little things going wrong can lead to big problems.

Another big lesson I learned had to do with honesty. One Sunday Ray picked me to help him with something new. It was a Sunday afternoon, and people were lined up from both windows to the curb. He handed me a pad of menus and said, "You take a line and I'll take a line. We'll check off what people want to order on a menu sheet. Then we'll give them the sheet, so they don't waste time placing their orders when they get to the window."

I got another case of stage fright. After I had helped about four people, I looked over and saw Ray was way ahead of me. I tried to go faster but made a lot of mistakes with the special orders—no onion on this one, no pickle on that one. When the orders I'd written started coming up, people began complaining. One of the guys at the window said, "You're gonna get fired now." He was joking, but I thought he was serious.

Finally, Ray came over to me and asked, "What happened?"

I was close to tears, my voice quivering. "Can I be truthful? You made me a nervous wreck. You were so far ahead, I just blew it trying to keep up. I'm sorry." I was so embarrassed. I had never made mistakes like that before. I waited for him to jump down my throat. Instead he just smiled because I had truthfully admitted I was in over my head.

That experience taught me something I used throughout my career as a trainer of electricians. I was the first employee of Huen Electric, a company that grew to 600 employees and almost $200 million a year in annual revenue. I always told my electricians, "Level with me. It'll be easier if you tell me the truth, because if you lie to me now, I've got an even bigger problem." On big electrical jobs, if there was a major foul-up, I'd say, "Everybody wants to blame somebody else, but we're not doing that.

 Let's fix the problem first, and then we'll talk later about what happened." You've got to let people know that as long as they're honest and do their best, they shouldn't fear getting into trouble for making a mistake.

I often invoked Ray Kroc when I did my leadership training. I preached all along that when you start the job you have to be totally organized. Using Ray as an example, I explained how he started his business from scratch on borrowed money. He had everything on the line when he went into business, and I said, "So do you guys. If you mess up here, and we lose, you lose. You lose your job and your reputation. You need to envision this job going smoothly, being profitable, and having everybody accountable, as Ray did."

I worked my way up to superintendent and was offered a promotion to project manager in the office. I chose to stay out in the excitement of the field, with the meetings and the yelling and screaming. I loved it. At times I felt I was getting dirty in the trenches, exactly what Ray Kroc did.

I never forgot my days at McDonald's. I live a mile away from the original restaurant. Three or four times a summer I'll drive over there with my lunch and park. I look at that museum while I quietly sit and eat my lunch, and it all comes back to me.

Years ago, I heard Ray Kroc on a call-in radio show while I was driving. I wanted so much to call, but that was before cell phones. I'm sure he would have remembered my stories and some of the funny things that happened that upset him. A few months afterward, he passed away. I was sad about missing that opportunity, but I'm always grateful for the opportunity I had to learn at his side.

DID YOU KNOW?

Ray Kroc's first McDonald's restaurant in Des Plaines was restored to its original form and reopened as a museum on May 21, 1985.

1956: Elvis Presley hits US music charts for the first time with "Heartbreak Hotel."

Phillip E. Rosner, PhD

AUTHOR'S NOTE

Team building is a core concept in business today. Back when Phil Rosner worked at a McDonald's for a summer, no one had to explain it or put a name on it. He went on to become an industrial psychologist, helping large corporations solve problems like team building, and he often drew upon what he learned on a McDonald's crew to do it. While working on that crew, he discovered that he enjoyed working with people, which influenced his decision to choose a career helping others. The discipline he learned helped him get through graduate school.

Dignity came from what you did, not where you worked.

At the start of that summer, when I was sixteen years old, I asked around at school who was hiring. The answer was McDonald's, so I applied at a restaurant, which is still there, in Skokie, Illinois, on Niles Center Road and Dempster Street. I was rather proud of the fact that I had found a real job. There was no negative connotation about working at McDonald's. In those days, dignity came from what you did, not where you worked.

New hires started with cleaning up. The second thing they taught me was how to prepare the potatoes for the French fries. Nowadays, you open a package of frozen fries and pour them into the deep fryer. Back then, you started with raw potatoes. We washed them, skinned them, sliced them, then blanched them before they went into the fryer. Because it was all done by hand in the restaurant daily, it took a while.

The first mistake I made was taking advantage of the fact that you could eat anything you wanted anytime and as much as you wanted. The first day, I was making triple and quadruple cheeseburgers. I got so sick.

Although I worked there just one summer, I learned a lot about the importance of process. When we were told to run forty-eight hamburgers at once, we didn't do it just right to left. We did it left to right and back to front. We had a hand dispenser with mustard on one side and ketchup on the other and gave it exactly two squeezes. You learned to always follow the steps in order.

My manager was a real mentor—he exemplified all the things you're supposed to do when you're dealing with young people. He was fair, he listened to you, and he avoided putting you under any pressure, even when correcting your behavior. For example, two people might squabble over whose turn it was to do a chore. He had to deal with those kinds of little arguments and figure out some way to make it fair so that everybody was happy with no bad feelings.

That was my first exposure to a team-management style. When I first started reading about team development theory, it seemed familiar to me. Then when I became a team developer in my career and started doing it, I realized that I had actually learned it in 1959 at McDonald's.

Team development was done subtly at McDonald's. For example, the manager made a point of keeping the same people on the same shifts, so we got used to working with the same people every day. He was very clear that we each had a job, that it was *our* job, and we were responsible for it. But we learned that the whole unit performed better if you helped out when one of the team members needed it. If someone fell behind on a task and you were done with your tasks, you lent a hand. There was no such thing as, "That's not my job." You took responsibility for the whole team.

The manager encouraged this by saying, "Joe could use a little help. If you've finished with what you were doing, could you help him out?" I heard that two or three times in the first week. By the last time I heard it, I knew that one of my jobs was to look around and see if anybody else needed anything. I don't recall ever hearing the word *team*, but that's what it was. This was before the consultancy business got big and everybody had to have a name for things. Back then, it was just the way to do it.

The reward systems were a lot different then, too. For example, if you were working a closing shift, you had to close out, clean up for the day, and get everything ready for the next day, leaving everything spotless. This really helped me learn the discipline that I lacked as a teenager. If the team worked efficiently to get it done, we got what we considered a tremendous reward. The manager would say, "Well done." We would look at each other and just smile. If he didn't say it, we knew we had to try harder.

1959

Mattel launches Barbie Doll. Boeing launches 707.

From my perspective as a psychologist, I know that the reward system forces you to figure out what the behavior is that gets rewarded. So you start monitoring yourself to see if you're doing what you're supposed to be doing that tends to get you the reward. That's what we psychologists help people do—work independently and self-monitor.

Another valuable lesson I learned from my short stint at McDonald's was how to deal with customers. We got some really bizarre, unpleasant customers sometimes, but we were expected to treat them like kings and queens. One of my coworkers once complained that a customer was wrong about something. The manager corrected him by saying, "The customer is not always right but is always treated like he's right."

I put this lesson to use once when a customer ordered a hamburger. When I gave it to him, he claimed he'd ordered a cheeseburger. I could have said, "No, sir, you ordered a hamburger," but instead I had learned to say, "Oh, I'm terribly sorry. I'm certain that's my mistake. Let me give you what you wanted." The manager later paid me a compliment for that.

I brought to future jobs what I'd learned at McDonald's about teamwork and customer service. McDonald's is where I learned that I really liked dealing with the public. I never would have imagined I would enjoy working the window and dealing with the money.

A couple of years later, as a college freshman, I worked in the toy department at a department store in Skokie called The Fair Store. That year the store had Shootin' Shell cap pistols, the most popular toy for boys. They had little pellets that fit into the little jackets. You actually loaded the gun, and it would shoot out the front.

When I got to The Fair Store, it wasn't twenty minutes before I realized that everyone was asking about the guns. I had all the guys in the toy department strap on a toy gun. When someone asked, "What's all this about the Shootin' Shell cap pistol?" I replied, "Watch." Then another salesman and I drew and shot at each other. We sold out of those things every week and had a good time.

High school and college were relatively easy for me, and I got very good grades. When I got to graduate school, I found it to be a bit harder. When I failed my first graduate statistics exam, I thought, "Remember what you learned in your previous jobs." Discipline was the key, figuring out what to do step by step, just like frying the burgers or making the fries at McDonald's. I was determined to get on track and started a seven-day program, getting back to discipline. If I hadn't, I'm sure I wouldn't have graduated.

One of my favorite anecdotes about how my experience informed my career as an organizational psychologist was when I worked on a project with a Fortune 100 telecom company. There were about thirty middle-level managers who were struggling with the teamwork concept. It was costing the company a fortune. We were doing a very large team-building project that went on for about eight months. One day I was sitting in a meeting as a nonparticipating observer and a manager was talking about having missed a deadline and being in danger of making a customer unhappy.

I raised my hand and said, "You told us that the guy on the other team didn't get you the information you needed on time because he didn't have enough people to help. But you had three or four people on your team with nothing to do."

"That's correct," the manager said.

"You knew that if he didn't give it to you on time, you were not going to get your own tasks done on time, so why didn't you ask him if he could use a couple of your people to help?"

They looked at me like that was the dumbest idea in the world. They explained that to make it happen, they would have had to ask the home office for permission then fill out forms detailing the time of the people on loan, for bookkeeping purposes.

It's too bad bureaucracy gets in the way of common sense sometimes. I explained that if they were helpful to someone else today, it could benefit them when they needed help in the future. If one member of the team fails, the whole team fails. It was so bizarre that I had to explain this concept to these well-paid managers at this huge corporation. They acted as if that were the first time they were learning this lesson—something I'd learned when I was sixteen years old at McDonald's.

DID YOU KNOW?

1959: McDonald's began billboard advertising. McDonald's opened its one hundredth store in Fond Du Lac, Wisconsin.

1960s

HIRED 1965

Frank J. Sandoval

AUTHOR'S NOTE

Frank Sandoval is the first person in this book who started as crew and ended up being an owner/operator. As of this writing, his company owns fourteen restaurants in Colorado—two of them owned by his older son. He is noteworthy for being one of the first franchisees of Hispanic heritage and one of the youngest when he started. He comes from a modest background and is a great example of a group represented by many others in this book who achieved a remarkable degree of success starting from an entry-level position.

You're going to have a key person or persons who will help you, and you need to take care of them.

The summer between my sophomore and junior years in high school in Pueblo, Colorado, my parents wanted me to have a real job for the summer instead of the odd jobs I had done before, like mowing lawns. They had been hard workers all their lives and wanted me to get good experience. My mother had been a maid, and my father had completed an army career that included a tour in Korea driving tanks. After that he worked in a local steel mill.

Being a bag boy at the local supermarket seemed like it might be fun, so I asked my parents to drive me there to fill out the application. When I came back out to the car, I ran into a school friend who was coming out of the McDonald's across the street. He was excited. "I just got hired!"

My parents told me I should apply but I had my mind set on the grocery store job. They were adamant, so I reluctantly went in and was hired on the spot. I came out with all my paperwork and instructions on what to do and when to report. That's how I started my career, by unwillingly applying at McDonald's.

Once I started working there, I discovered that I really enjoyed the atmosphere and the camaraderie. I still have very fond memories of those early years. Most of the people working there at night with me were young. During the day, there were older, more mature employees— housewives and second-shift workers who wanted extra income.

I started out in the milkshake station. From there I went to the front counter. I found the counter more challenging because I was a shy kid, but with training and experience, I became very outgoing and learned to love talking to customers. It ended up being my favorite station to work. Working at McDonald's definitely brought me out of my shell. It was fun being an ambassador for the brand.

One of my biggest challenges was balancing work and school. I was just a fair student, and when I began to work, I struggled to maintain my grades. I loved working and didn't particularly enjoy going to school. I wished I could have quit school and just worked, but my parents wouldn't allow it.

In those days, nobody talked about working at McDonald's as a dead-end job. In fact, it was a cool place to work. The football players, cheerleaders, and popular kids were part of the crew. I made a lot of friends and advanced quickly. It was like a game, everybody pulling together trying to break the restaurant's previous sales records. People were in awe that we could sell hamburgers, fries, and shakes for the price that we did. In that town, McDonald's was seen as a class organization.

One of the more difficult challenges was dealing with my friends who thought they would get free food. I was confronted with that a lot, and it was hard having to always say, "No, no, no." I didn't want to lose my job. It was a valuable business lesson about keeping your friendships separate from your business. I found that to be even more important when I got into the management development program. By the age of nineteen, I was counseling my peers as well as people who were much older than I was.

There was a gentleman who worked the grill who was married with children. He worked at the state hospital full time, and then he came to McDonald's, worked the lunch rush, and went home to bed. He was habitually ten to fifteen minutes late at a time of day when we needed all hands on deck. I sat down with him and emphasized how he was letting the team down and how it was affecting the rest of us. It worked. He started showing up on time after that. He was a success story.

The outcomes weren't always so great. There was a young man who was a friend of mine, about my age, who was one of the fastest employees, but he took shortcuts. Everything we do is systematic, so if you cut out a step, it's going to affect you somewhere else. He worked so fast that he tore the meat patties when he turned them, and he scattered the whole grill with the salt mix instead of making sure every patty got the proper seasoning. He was faster than the other grill people, but he wasn't delivering the product that we wanted. I sat him down and explained that he had to follow the steps, even if it meant slowing down, because we needed to deliver a consistent product. He never got it. It wasn't an easy thing to do, especially at that age, but I had to fire him.

One of my proudest moments was when I was promoted to assistant manager and I got to wear a red hat that distinguished me from the crew, who wore white hats. It was just a paper hat that I threw away at the end of my shift, but to me it was a career high point. I was only nineteen years old and was managing a busy restaurant.

My parents were delighted with how I had blossomed, commenting on how quickly I was maturing, accepting responsibility, and gaining confidence. They were proud of me, but they wanted me to go on to college. I started out studying to become a schoolteacher at Southern Colorado State. The tuition was low, I lived at home, and I was able to continue working at McDonald's.

My boss was the owner/operator Carter Farrar, Sr., a businessman from Los Angeles. He had become a franchisee because he owned a piece of real estate in Boulder, Colorado, a suburb of Denver. Ray Kroc wanted the land for a new restaurant, but Carter wasn't interested in selling. Ray was determined and won him over by persuading him to invest in a franchise restaurant. That later led to a deal that gave Carter a territorial license covering Pueblo County.

Over the years, I progressed through the chain of command. When I was promoted to supervisor at age twenty, I began to develop a close professional relationship with Carter. As a supervisor responsible for more than one restaurant, we spoke by phone every Sunday for an hour or more. I had to report sales, transactions, profits, problems that may have developed, and the results of occasional inspections from the corporation. I became so close to him over the years that it felt as though we were related.

1965

Bill Cosby, starring in *I Spy*, becomes the first African American to headline a television show.

I was still in college when Carter offered me the opportunity to purchase his original restaurant in Wheat Ridge. There was no way I could manage the purchase financially, but he said, "I just need to know that this is something you'd like to do. If it is, I'll work out the details."

"I can't imagine anything I'd rather do," I told him. But I was nervous, afraid of failing. My father sat down with me for a talk one night.

"You know, son, some guys just aren't meant to be the top boss. Some guys are meant to always have someone giving them direction. Maybe you shouldn't be the top guy." His reverse psychology worked, but Carter had to fight hard to get corporate approval for me to buy the franchise. I'm forever grateful that he didn't give up on me, for in 1978 I became one of the first franchisees of Hispanic heritage.

When we finally got the deal done, Carter shared with me some pearls of wisdom: "This business will eat you up if you don't learn to balance your life. You can easily find yourself working day and night. Learn to prioritize: family, work, and whatever else is important to you."

He also said, "Pay it forward, and take care of the people who help you become successful. During your career, you're going to have a key person or persons that will help you, and you need to take care of them as I have done for you." I have tried to keep that promise and one of my early employees from my first franchise, Rick Hill, is today owner/operator of six McDonald's restaurants—three of which I sold to him.

Over the course of my career, I've been honored numerous times with awards for business and leadership, but I'm proudest of the McDonald's Golden Arch Award I won in 1981. And in 2006 I was invited to the White House for their Hispanic Heritage Month celebration, where I and other Hispanic business and community leaders were honored for our contributions to society.

Every day I live Carter's advice to pay it forward. All of my managers start as crew and are promoted from within. Treating my employees like family leads to more productive, loyal managers. My own family is involved in the business, too. My wife of forty-three years, Virginia, has supported my work with McDonald's every step of the way.

My older son, Mitchell, was just approved by the corporation and is now an owner/operator of two restaurants. My younger son, Michael, came into the company recently, is an area supervisor, and hopes to be a franchisee someday too. Both are college graduates and had a chance to work for a while before choosing to come into the business with me.

In a way, my parents became part of the McDonald's family too. I named my company Clara Corporation after my mother. My parents framed the first check issued by Clara Corporation, and when they were alive it hung on the wall of their bedroom. They were so proud of me.

My father even sent me a check for $1,000 every time I opened a new restaurant, just to "help out." They came to each of my grand openings and I gave them the first dollar that came in across every counter. They put all those dollars in the frame with my company's first check.

LEE STRANAHAN

HIRED 1966

Jay Leno

AUTHOR'S NOTE

There are many celebrities whose first real job was under the Golden Arches, but Jay Leno may be the most recognizable. Like others of lesser fame who have gone on to successful careers in other fields, Jay connects the dots from the experiences he had as a teenager with his career path and even his management philosophy. And, of course, he tells a few good stories.

Promoting from within is a lesson I took with me from McDonald's to The Tonight Show.

After I started working at McDonald's in Andover, Massachusetts, the school guidance counselor called my mom in for a meeting one day to discuss my grades. I was dyslexic as a kid and not great in school.

The guidance counselor said, "Mrs. Leno, have you ever thought of taking Jay out of school?"

My mother looked a little shocked. "Out of school? No. Why?"

He said, "Well, he's kind of disruptive, and he doesn't really do that well."

"I'd like him to finish high school, at least."

"Well, you know, he works at McDonald's," the counselor said, "and they have a wonderful program at McDonald's Hamburger University."

My mother wasn't convinced. "That's very nice, but still, I want him to at least finish high school." I did, and I even graduated from college.

I was the kid who always wanted to work. To me, being a kid meant I had two dollars and everything cost three, so I wanted to have a job and earn money. McDonald's was a great job for that, and I loved it. I worked at a restaurant on Main Street for two years, from 1966 to 1968. This was back in the good old days when they still had roast beef and strawberry shortcake, which I was a huge fan of. I earned whatever the minimum wage was, but I saved enough to be able to buy a two-year-old 1965 Buick Gran Sport 401 four-speed in my senior year. I had at least as nice a car as my dad, which was kind of funny.

My mother wasn't too happy about my guidance counselor's suggestion that I leave high school and go work at McDonald's full time. But she was all for me working at McDonald's while I finished school. My parents were both very supportive. I think they liked the idea that they could pass by the restaurant, look in, see me there, and know that everything was okay. I wasn't in the back of a warehouse somewhere sweeping up. I was behind this counter on Main Street, and my parents could drive by and say, "Okay, he's still there. I can see him."

There are a few ways that working there left a big impression on me. One of my favorite stories about McDonald's has to do with a sack of potatoes and a pair of underpants.

In those days, the French fries had to be made from scratch. We had to cut what seemed like a ton of potatoes every day. You'd pick up the potato, put it in the cutter, squeeze it, and out would come French fries. I had these massive forearms from cutting those potatoes.

One day when I was getting ready to cut the potatoes, I went into the store room to get a fresh sack. Tom Curtin, the owner/operator, was with me and there, on top of the sack of potatoes, was a pair of underpants. Sometimes crew members changed into their uniforms at work and somebody had apparently forgotten their underpants.

I expected Tom to tell me to throw out the top layer of potatoes and wash the rest. Instead he said, simply, "Get rid of all those potatoes."

"Really?" That was very impressive to me.

"Get rid of that whole batch. Just get rid of all of it." So the standards for quality were quite high. It was one of those life lessons I never forgot.

Another thing that always impressed me about McDonald's was that everybody in the company had come up through the company. I remember in the early years after I had been on TV a few times, I was at a McDonald's convention, and guys were walking around the hotel in their blue blazers with the McDonald's patch on the pocket. They were not embarrassed at all.

Everyone I spoke to had started out as a crew person, like me, washing floors and cutting potatoes. They learned the business from the ground up. From taking the orders to doing the accounting, they knew every facet of the business, much like a good mechanic knows every facet of a car. I was impressed with their knowledge of and loyalty to the company.

1966

First *Star Trek* episode, "The Man Trap," is broadcast on Sept. 8, about a creature that sucks salt from human bodies.

Promoting from within is something I brought with me to *The Tonight Show*. Our executive producer started out as an intern and wound up being producer of the show. Most everybody on this show started out in a lower position than where they are now. That's a lesson that I took from McDonald's.

The fun part of working at McDonald's was getting there before the restaurant opened. We'd fire up the grill and take ten to fifteen patties and make giant burgers for ourselves. We got caught doing it, and that came to an end fairly quickly. But we didn't get fired for that. Kid stuff was kid stuff. You got fired for dishonesty or stealing, not kids' stuff like joking around.

One day, as a joke, I went to school with my uniform on—the black shoes, black pants, white shirt, apron, and hat. I remember sitting in class and the teacher said, "Mr. Leno, what are you doing?"

"I have to go to work right after school," I replied.

"Really? And you have to wear your uniform all day?"

"I don't have time to change."

"All right, get out. Get out!" She sent me down to the principal's office, and my mom had to come down with a shirt so I could change.

When I worked for Mr. Curtin, he said, "You know, you're always joking around. You should be a counter man. Maybe keep the customers happy and get a few laughs." He put me on the counter, and that's where I really belonged. I kidded around with everybody and pulled the usual kid stunts. My friends would come in and say, "Can I have fifteen burgers and ten orders of fries?"

"That'll be a dollar!"

Finally, one day, Mr. Curtin said, "You know, the restaurant lost $25,000 last month. Have you guys been giving out a lot of food?"

I shrugged and pulled a face. "Ah . . . not me. No." So I had to learn my lesson there: no friends-and-family discount.

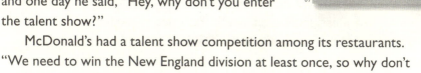

But he saw something in me, personality-wise, and one day he said, "Hey, why don't you enter the talent show?"

McDonald's had a talent show competition among its restaurants. "We need to win the New England division at least once, so why don't you do a comedy skit or something?"

I said, "Okay, I'll do that."

I did a comedy routine with another guy, and we won. I got a camera and a trip to the Bahamas, and I thought, "Wow, maybe this could be something good!" I wasn't great in school, but this was something I was good at.

So McDonald's is sort of what got me into show business.

HIRED 1966

Henry "Hank" James Thomas

AUTHOR'S NOTE

For many minorities, McDonald's has provided opportunities they might not have had otherwise. Henry "Hank" Thomas is a historic example. A college student at Howard University, he volunteered in 1961 to become a Freedom Rider, engaging in civil disobedience protests against segregated public facilities throughout the South and very nearly getting himself killed by vigilantes. Then he earned a Purple Heart as a medic in the Vietnam War. Given a chance to prove himself at a McDonald's restaurant in Washington, DC, he went on to build a family business that has included multiple McDonald's franchises and a group of hotels in the Atlanta area. Today he is celebrated as a hero of the civil rights movement and serves as a role model in the African-American community.

"They wouldn't let him operate the register,
so he bought the restaurant!"

Although I grew up very, very poor, I always assumed that the
conditions I lived in were not the conditions I was supposed to
live in, even though that was the normal state for black folks at
that time. From early on, some of my favorite readings have always been
people who have risen above their circumstances. Most of the people
that I read about were white, but I assumed that was the way I was going
to do it as well.

My mother only got as far as the sixth grade, but she taught me how
to read at a very early age. She would always say, "If you get an education,
that's something they can't take away from you." The oldest of eleven
kids, I was very competitive. I always wanted to be the smartest one in
the class and was always raising my hand so I could show the teacher how
much I knew.

Part of my childhood I lived in Georgia, in an area dominated by the
Ku Klux Klan. My school was segregated and only went to the eleventh
grade. Classes didn't start for us until November because we black kids
had to be available to pick cotton and help the white farmers gather in the
crops.

In 1960, against the odds for a black teenager just out of high school,
I got attend Howard University in Washington, DC, the most prestigious
historically African-American college in the country. The student civil
rights movement was just getting started and I participated in sit-ins at
segregated facilities in Virginia and Maryland, joined by white students
from nearby American University.

When a call went out from the Congress of Racial Equality, CORE, for
volunteers to participate in the Freedom Rides I was only nineteen and
too young. But I was a big fellow and bluffed my way through. I became
one of the original thirteen Freedom Riders who rode on a bus through
the Deep South, getting arrested nearly two dozen times for trying to eat
at white lunch counters, use white waiting rooms in bus stations, and the
like.

Sit-ins were a fairly dangerous activity and the second time I was
arrested was back in my hometown of St. Augustine, Florida, in July 1960.
I went down to the local five-and-dime and had a one-man sit-in. The
authorities tried to have me declared insane. The psychiatrist refused to

go along with them, otherwise I don't know how long I would have been locked up in a mental hospital.

My mother was absolutely horrified. I had never been in trouble, always known as a nice boy. She came to visit me in jail and pleaded with the jailers to let me go and prayed quite expressively. It was embarrassing because here I was a revolutionary and my mother was trying to rescue me. Eventually I was bailed out by Sammy Davis, Jr., the entertainer.

I came closest to death in Winnsboro, South Carolina, where I had been arrested for a sit-in. The police took me out of jail that night and I thought they were driving me to the bus station so that I could leave, but instead they took me to a Klan gathering. They pointed their guns at me and said, "Get out of the car." I had to run for my life. Just in the nick of time, a black minister, a World War II veteran who was a paraplegic, drove up in his car and told me to jump in. He saved my life and was indeed the bravest man that I have ever known.

The conflict in Vietnam was heating up and one way they dealt with troublemakers like me was to draft us into the Army. I was drafted in 1963, trained as a medic, and ended up in Vietnam where, in April 1966, I was caught in an ambush and ended up with a badly shattered arm. I was sent home to Walter Reed Army Hospital back in Washington for treatment.

There was a McDonald's down the street from the hospital, on Georgia Avenue. I stopped in there one day and was fascinated to find that all the people working there were black. I'd never seen anything like it, plus the food was good and inexpensive.

I asked about a part-time job. The guy looked at the big cast on my right arm and hand. "How are you going to do this?"

"You must have something around here that I could do. Try me out. If it doesn't work, don't pay me." I worked at the bun toaster and was very conscientious about it. Within a couple of weeks they gave me a nickel raise, so I hit the big time, making $1.30 an hour.

Most of the people in that restaurant were part-timers and a lot of the fellows were school teachers who needed help paying their bills. They were a highly motivated and intelligent crew, and especially kind to me. They called me Soldier Boy and John Wayne. I only spent a few months there, but it was a wonderful time.

Two white men owned that restaurant, but the manager was black. That fascinated me, coming out of the culture of the South where black folks weren't in charge of anything, let alone a business owned by white people. I asked the manager, "How in the world could I get to be a manager?" He took the time to talk to me and showed me as much as I wanted to learn.

I recognized what a good business it was and even though it seemed like an impossibility at the time, the idea of owning one intrigued me.

After I was discharged from the hospital, I moved to Atlanta, Georgia, with my wife and child and became a fireman for the Atlanta Fire Department. I also had a part-time business putting coin-operated washers and dryers in the basements of apartment buildings and splitting the proceeds with the owners.

I still needed to do some part-time work, so I went to a McDonald's on Gresham Avenue and was hired because I had experience. I started in the kitchen. One day, when we were extremely busy, I went up front to help out. I will never forget this one customer, a white guy, who would not give me his order. Here I was, just returned from Vietnam, just getting over my injuries, and this guy was saying, "I don't want you waiting on me."

> **1966**
> Avg. cost of new house
> $14,200
> Avg. annual income
> $6,900
> Gas per gallon 32 cents

The next day, I asked the manager to put me on a register. He hemmed and hawed and finally said, "I'd like to do it, Hank, but these people will walk out of here."

"Are you kidding me?" I was filled with righteous indignation. "Had it not been for this injury, I would be flying a helicopter in Vietnam. And these folks don't want me to work a cash register?"

He shrugged. "I'm sorry."

Later, a local newspaper did a story about people who had full-time jobs and ran part-time businesses. I was one of those people featured and after it appeared I got a call from the Burger King people asking me if I would be interested in becoming a franchisee. They were making an effort to diversify, so I did become a franchisee.

From there I was able to buy a McDonald's franchise in Atlanta, Georgia. Later I bought the restaurant where the manager wouldn't put me on the register. The local television station came out and did a story, saying, "They wouldn't let him operate the register, so he bought the restaurant."

Altogether, my wife and I have owned six McDonald's. A few years ago, we thought we were going to retire and sold all but one, which her sister and brother-in-law were operating. Then I got bored with retirement, and she bought two more. Right now we own three and I own an interest in three Marriott Hotels, too.

My mother will be ninety years old in 2012 and she still gets carried away sometimes, like she did when I got arrested. She tells people how proud she is of her son's Freedom Riders. I have to pull her aside and say, "Mother, I did not organize the Freedom Rides. They were not *my* Freedom Riders."

DID YOU KNOW?

1966: The hot apple pie was being test marketed.

HIRED 1967

Andrew H. Card, Jr.

AUTHOR'S NOTE

Andrew Card was a young husband, father, and college student when he began his three years working at a McDonald's in Columbia, South Carolina. Being slightly older and more settled than most of the crew, he fell into a leadership role. He enjoyed mentoring and serving as an example for others, along the way teaching a young man a surprising lesson about integrity. He recalls developing instincts that served him well in his career, including five and a half years in the White House as President George W. Bush's chief of staff. Nicknamed "Iron Man," the *Washington Post* said that Card ran "the most buttoned-down, leak-proof, on-task, on-time, on-message White House in history." Card would later say that running the White House was like working a fast-food counter during a lunch hour rush that never ends.

McDonald's was unique as a great equalizer. Wealthy and poor, black and white all came to McDonald's and stood in the same lines and sat at the same booths.

S ome reports mistakenly have me down as having worked at McDonald's twice—in high school and again in college. I *tried* to get a job at McDonald's in high school, but the competition was too stiff. It was a cool thing to work at any quick-service restaurant in those days, so I got a job at a competitor.

My first experience in the restaurant business was as the toddler son of a janitor, sleeping on a banquette in Howard Johnson's restaurants late at night while my teenaged father worked. My parents eventually had five children and worked long hours to make ends meet and allow my father to earn his college degree and then go on to law school.

All of us kids were expected to work, and we did. I delivered newspapers seven days a week in my home town of Holbrook, Massachusetts, until I was old enough to work in a restaurant. My goal was to save enough so that, with scholarships, my education wouldn't cost my parents anything.

I went to the University of South Carolina, where I pursued an engineering degree. By then, I was married. We were starting our family, and I needed a job. I was recruited to work at a Hardee's by a friend. I was a McDonald's fan, so I applied there, was hired, and started off at eight-five cents an hour plus all I could eat during my breaks. I took full advantage of that benefit.

I was scared to death at first. I wanted to be responsible and provide for my wife and kids, so I really needed that job. It turned out to be a perfect fit. I could work as many hours as I wanted on a flexible schedule. During school breaks they'd let me pile them on.

I started off working at the window. We had real cash registers, not computers, so you had to do the math yourself. I was an engineering student, so I turned it into a math challenge. How quickly could I add up the total and get it right?

Our busy restaurant was often chosen to test-market new products, and I remember when they introduced the Big Mac. At first I thought no one would be interested in them, but after I tried one, I said, "People are going to like these!"

About a year and a half after I started, they promoted me to night manager. That was a big deal—I got a raise and had a significant management role. I was responsible for making sure the place was scrubbed from top to bottom at the end of each day. I always encouraged the kids to take pride in their work and enjoyed being a mentor.

I remember thinking that McDonald's was unique as a great equalizer. Wealthy and poor, black and white all came to McDonald's and stood in the same lines and sat at the same booths. The fact that the restaurant was integrated was somewhat novel for South Carolinians at the time. For me, coming from New England, the fact that it was novel was a shock.

One of the most memorable experiences happened during one of those night shifts. One of the young crew members was a bit of a tough kid with an attitude, but he worked well. One night I sent him to pick up the trash in the parking lot and happened to look out as he bent over, picked something up, and put it in his pocket.

1967
Thurgood Marshall sworn in as first black US Supreme Court justice.

When he came back in, I was doing the books for the day and asked him, "Did you find something out there?"

"Uh, nope."

"Are you sure you didn't find something out there?"

He blushed, shrugged, and pulled a wallet from his pocket. It had some money and an ID in it. The owner was from Atlanta, Georgia.

"Okay," I said, "Write a note, put it in an envelope, and we'll send him the wallet."

I made him sit down and write it then and there, and I mailed it the next day. The fellow quit after a few months and moved away, so I forgot the incident.

About a year later, I was working at the restaurant one night and the same fellow showed up.

"What have you been up to?" I asked. "What brings you to town?"

He reminded me about the wallet and said, "I wanted to thank you for teaching me a good lesson. Let me tell you what happened. Some time later, I got a letter thanking me for returning the wallet and informing me that the guy had died, leaving me $2,000 in his will."

Through observation I came to realize that if someone didn't like his responsibilities or the task didn't fit his skills, he would not succeed. If somebody wanted to work at the window but was poor with math and took too long to make change, they didn't succeed. Others lacked the hand-eye coordination to work the grill. They were slow or often got burned. Others were great at watching the fries or cleaning the vats.

So a big part of my job was determining how I could help each kid succeed at a task, because then he or she would like it more and work harder. If someone working the register was being brusque with the customers, I would say, "Want to try working the fries? Want to try the grill?"

When I graduated with my engineering degree in January of 1971, I was offered a chance to be the manager of a new McDonald's in Florence, South Carolina. The franchisee who owned the restaurant I worked in also owned that one. It was an attractive situation, and I came close to accepting. But in the end the pull of our roots prevailed and we moved back to Massachusetts to start my new career as an engineer.

Years later, when my first daughter was old enough, my wife and I decided she needed some real life experience and suggested she work at McDonald's to get it. Did she need to work for the money? Probably not. Did she need to work to learn *how* to work? Absolutely. In the end, she preferred the Roy Rogers uniforms, with the cowboy hats, so that's where she got her experience. We still laugh about that hat today.

DID YOU KNOW?

In 1967, test marketing began for the Big Mac sandwich, developed by owner/operator Jim Delligatti. It was introduced on the national menu the following year and sold for forty-five cents. Currently the Big Mac is sold in more than 100 countries.

HIRED 1967

Marcia L. Fudge

AUTHOR'S NOTE

To be successful in the restaurant business, it helps to have a flair for dealing with many different kinds of people. That proved to be good training for Marcia Fudge in her later career in public service. After getting her law degree, she served as a prosecutor, county finance official, mayor of Warrensville Heights, Ohio, and today represents the Eleventh District of Ohio in Congress.

Decent work is never beneath anybody.

When McDonald's opened its first restaurant on Cleveland's east side, it felt like our neighborhood had arrived. The restaurant was brand new in the community and a novelty, the first place where you could walk up to the window and get a meal or a snack to go. My association came through my cousin, who was hired to be the manager. I started working there before I was even fifteen.

Because it was the first McDonald's in the neighborhood, we always wanted people to know that we were the most professional, cleanest restaurant where they would feel very comfortable. We took a great deal of pride in how that restaurant looked, how we looked, and how we addressed the public. If you didn't do it right, you didn't stay on crew for long.

If somebody didn't show up to work, we stayed to work their shift. It wouldn't happen today, but back then I could volunteer to work a fourteen-hour day. After we'd shut the restaurant down we'd clean up, mop, scrub the grill—whatever needed to be done, we did it. No one ever said, "This isn't part of my job description." We just did whatever it took because we wanted it to be successful. We wanted that place to be the best.

Being the only restaurant of its type in the area, lunch was busy. We kids made it a game to try and get each customer out the door in three minutes. We worked out routines to keep people entertained while they waited for their food. We yelled out orders, danced around, sang silly songs, and competed to see who could bag meals the fastest. The customers loved it, and many of them came in regularly to see what kind of routine we'd come up with that day.

I grew up in a fairly poor neighborhood, with my divorced mother working hard to provide for my brother and me. Getting my own paycheck meant a great deal to me. It meant not having to ask my mother for spending money. If I needed some little thing, I had the money to get it. Every day I went home smelling like French fries, but when I got those paychecks it felt like I had a million bucks.

I worked at McDonald's most of the way through high school, in the afternoons and on weekends. My responsibilities increased, and when I was seventeen, if a manager wasn't there or was busy, I could step in. Sometimes I'd have to make tough decisions, like sending someone home for misbehaving. It's still challenging for me to deal with someone who makes mistakes, but I've had experience doing it since I was a teenager. Back then, it was just part of my job, but when I think about it now, I realize how significant it was to give a teenage girl like me so much responsibility.

The owner/operator and manager believed that everyone deserved an opportunity to work. We hired a lot of people who were in need of a second chance. I remember our night manager—probably in her thirties—had some family and dependence issues. We helped support her in her emotional and family issues until she could get herself straight and start to figure out how to handle her paycheck. I had a good knowledge of money as a kid, so I helped her on paydays with her budgeting.

My cousin made the purchasing decisions for the restaurant and because I was good in math, he asked me to help him out. After working at the counter for a while, I knew what sold and what didn't. I may not have been able to say, "You need to order exactly this many burgers," but I knew that the cheeseburgers sold faster than the hamburgers, so I could suggest that he order more cheese.

Working at the restaurant gave me the opportunity to do good work in a positive, supportive environment with people of all ages and from all backgrounds. The most important thing I learned was how to deal with the public. People are demanding when spending their money. If I made a mistake, I needed to correct it. I also learned to take pride in myself and my work.

If I were addressing a roomful of skeptical parents today, with children old enough to start working at a place like McDonald's, I would talk about the fact that good, decent work is never beneath anybody. People look down on what they might consider minimum-wage or fast food jobs. But it's always been my philosophy that it's better to work hard to earn something than to have it given to you.

We were young enough to believe that the world was going to reward us for all the work we did. As kids, we were always taught that if you do your best, it's good enough.

Don Armstrong

AUTHOR'S NOTE

Don Armstrong's story is one of unusual focus and persistence. He decided in high school he wanted to own a McDonald's franchise. It took him a decade and he met his share of obstacles along the way but refused to be dissuaded from his dreams. Today he owns one of the largest restaurant groups in the McDonald's system.

You know what made this company successful?
We had principles even when we were poor.
—Ray A. Kroc

The inspiration for my career came from the experience I had as a crew member in North Hollywood, California, on Burbank Boulevard. Up until I was old enough to work a real job, I had helped my father while he was doing home remodeling to supplement his income as a police officer. My aspirations were unformed, although I had thought about becoming an architectural engineer, experimented with drafting, and studied up on math.

When I turned sixteen, my father said he had seen a Help Wanted sign in the window of McDonald's and encouraged me to apply. I wasn't driving yet, so I put on my little brown suit and my tie, got a bit of interview coaching from my parents, and rode my ten-speed bicycle the three miles to McDonald's. Looking back, I was probably mistaken for a missionary in those days of beads, long hair, and tie-dyed T-shirts.

The person who interviewed me was the owner/operator, Bob Yervoseck, a boisterous, gruff guy who had previously worked in the oil fields. He hired me on the spot.

I quickly grew to admire Bob. He worked that restaurant from open to close, all day long. He could be funny, but he could also be strict. He established for me, in the way that he worked, acted, and felt about the business, a core value that appealed to me: never cut corners. He demonstrated that value in everything he did, right down to the smallest detail.

One of my favorite examples from early on had to do with product freshness. We made the hamburgers in the back, set them up on a tray, and then the person up front took the hamburgers off the tray, wrapped them in paper, and put them in a warming bin. There was a system for marking them so you knew how long it had been since they were cooked. There was a strict standard: ten minutes was as long as they could be in that warming bin. After ten minutes, you were supposed to throw the leftovers out, no matter how wasteful it seemed to us kids working there.

Bob came by the station one day and noticed a sandwich that had been in the warming bin for eleven or twelve minutes. He yelled at us, "What is it that you don't understand about ten minutes?" He grabbed a handful of hamburgers and threw them in the garbage. You'd think you would get in trouble for throwing away food. Instead, it was about food quality and making sure you did it right.

When I was ready to move up, I transferred to another restaurant, in Saugus, California, right out of high school, dreaming of one day being an owner/operator. I was still just a high school grad flipping hamburgers. Yet there was never any doubt in my mind that it was going to happen. I put in sixty to seventy hours a week, taking no time off.

My parents asked me two questions: "When are you going to get a real job?" and "Why would this guy who's got you working sixty to seventy hours a week making him money hand over fist want to see you leave or move up?"

No matter what anyone said, I believed it would happen. The operators I worked for—there were five in all—each became mentors and father figures. Exploitation was never a part of it. Don Dehoff gave me my big opportunity when I became his restaurant manager at twenty years old.

When I went to work for Jim Pegram in Sacramento in 1974, I told him I wanted to do a great job for him, but he needed to know that I was looking to be an owner one day, even though I didn't know how I was going to get there. He said, "I'll support you all the way. You'll be able to do it." He had sons working to get into the business, but he supported my ambitions as well.

1969

Man Walks
On Moon!

What I learned from Jim's approach was that by supporting me he ended up getting my best work, and much more. I wasn't just working for him, I was working for me, and he reaped the benefit of that.

In 1974, when I was twenty-two, I had the good fortune to be seated next to Ray Kroc at a manager's convention in San Francisco, and we exchanged a few words. At one point I went to the bathroom and he happened to walk in a moment later. We ended up at neighboring urinals and he said, out of the blue, "You know what made this business successful?"

I scrambled to remember what I'd learned: the points outlined in the training manual about service, quality, and cleanliness. I started to answer with a list when he interrupted me. "It was because we had principles when we were poor." That has stuck with me forever.

Each of the owner/operators I worked for influenced me in a significant way. The things they cared about in their businesses went beyond making hamburgers and dollars and cents.

When Jim Pegram had an operator review in 1977, he told the company he was working to get his sons into the business, but he also told them about my ambitions. After that meeting, he said the executive he'd met with was not encouraging. But Jim said, "Don't worry about it. That guy isn't going to be around by the time you're ready to go. You just keep doing what you're doing. The opportunity will present itself. All you've got to do is be ready when that happens."

Just as he predicted, everything changed in 1979 when the company began looking to expand by identifying successful managers who were ready to become operators. Interest rates were sky high, the economy was in the dumps, and raising the capital to purchase a franchise was difficult. The company introduced something called a business facilities lease that allowed people like me to put down a small amount of cash to lease a restaurant with an option to buy later. The objective was to expand into smaller markets.

The first restaurant I acquired that way was in Hermiston, Oregon, a town of 8,000. By 1996 I had two restaurants but my career was limited by the rural location I operated in. I was struggling financially in one of them and came to a point where I had to sell in order to go forward. It was a tough decision, but it ultimately sharpened my business skills and made me a stronger operator and leader. It taught me that not every decision leads to success.

As time progressed, I felt ready for the next challenge. In 1998, I had the opportunity to purchase six restaurants in Everett, Washington, from Mike Pegram, whose father was the owner/operator who had encouraged me back in the 1970s. My two McDonald's careers became connected by the father and the son.

Today I own thirteen McDonald's in the Portland, Oregon, area and have served as chairman of McDonald's National Leadership Council, an owner/operator group. I have done my best to pay my good fortune forward by encouraging and supporting the people who work for me. I want them to dream big, and I want to support them.

That includes my oldest son who was approved as an operator in 2011. I remember when he was a child working in the dining room of one of our first restaurants, wiping down tables and having a ball because he got to work in a restaurant and none of his friends could. That's a part of the McFamily DNA—the way we work and support each other, the relationships between the company and the owner/operators, the relationships we have with our people and with our customers. It's something that cannot be manufactured.

DID YOU KNOW?

Groundbreaking ceremonies held for new corporate headquarters in Oak Brook in 1969.

The average McDonald's used a ton of beef per week in 1969. Nationally, it took 765,000 head of cattle to produce the 90 million pounds of beef patties served.

HIRED 1969

Steve Plotkin

AUTHOR'S NOTE

Some of the people who started out as crew and are today officers of McDonald's have had especially long careers, giving them a unique perspective on how the company has evolved. Steve Plotkin started his journey forty-three years ago with no particular plan in mind, assuming one day he'd get a "real job." Today he has one—president of the West Division and the person to whom I report. He is responsible for nearly 4,300 restaurants and 647 franchisees covering six geographic regions in sixteen states, with about $9 billion in annual sales. That kind of continuity is rare in business but common at McDonald's. Steve in particular is known for developing and promoting people through the ranks. I am one of those people he has allowed to learn and grow as my career progressed.

We are always developing our people and moving them up the ladder, creating the next generation of leaders.

My first night as a fifteen-year-old crew member at a McDonald's in Milwaukee, Wisconsin, was a busy Friday. I was assigned to the soda fountain. All I did all night was pour Cokes, orange drinks, and whatever else we were selling back then. I remember going home with my white uniform shirt sticky with beverage syrup.

The next day I was assigned to load a device called a burger-flipper for the guy who was cooking on the grill. The patties were delivered fresh in boxes and it was my job to fill up a rack that held twenty-four burgers. Then the cook would take the rack and flip twenty-four burgers down on the grill at once. We had this rotation running, and all I did was load the rack over and over again. That night I went home with my white shirt covered with blood stains.

On Sunday, I was assigned to work the Multimixer, a five-headed blender. If you weren't good at manipulating those mixers, when you took the shake off it would splatter all over you. That day I went home with shake mix all over me.

My mother said, "Hey, they've got to give you some more shirts! I can't keep doing laundry every night."

That was my first weekend with McDonald's, forty-three years ago. Today, we do a lot of things differently, but the standards remain just as high. An early experience I've never forgotten was the day the owner of the restaurant showed up. I was making shakes. We had big cartons of mix, and when I was opening one he saw me grab the inside of the lip. He went ballistic on me—sanitation-wise, that's a big no-no. I learned very quickly that you've got to watch every little thing you do.

Back then there was no stigma attached to working at McDonald's. In fact, kids wanted to work there, so we got the cream of the crop. The high school I attended was right down the street, so the restaurant was staffed mostly with students and their friends. There was another group of people that worked the day shift. They were known as the "day ladies" because they tended to be adult women who could work when the rest of us were in school.

In my early days I found it rather easy to get fired, and I was, several times. We weren't quite as buttoned-down then as we are today. A lot of shenanigans went on, all fairly harmless. I got fired once for dumping leftover shakes in the manager's gas tank because we didn't like him. Another time I got fired for pouring four gallons of bleach down the grease trap. Cleaning the trap was so unpleasant the job was used as punishment. Pouring bleach down it was the wrong way to do it. The assistant manager fired me.

But each time I got fired, I just showed up the next day and was told, "Okay, punch in, you're good." Today, I might not be fired so quickly, but I hope people would be unlikely to pull stunts like that.

The next year, when I was a senior, my McDonald's job was part of a work-study program. I went to school until 11:30 a.m. and then I'd dash off to McDonald's in time to man the lunch shift. The high school had open lunch hours and the kids could go anywhere they wanted, so we'd get slammed.

From high school I went to the University of Wisconsin–Milwaukee but spent more time carousing than studying. McDonald's was after me to go into management, so I quit college and went into the restaurant business full time.

1969

Half a million people gather in a field in upstate New York for Woodstock Music Festival.

Two of my responsibilities were hiring and scheduling. I hired a young lady who I found attractive and scheduled her to work with me. One night she insisted on taking off a shift without permission, and I fired her for insubordination. Thankfully, her father called and got the manager to ask me to give her another chance. I did and we ended up getting married.

When I left college, I thought I might do something else. McDonald's was all I had done since I was fifteen. They wanted to start me out with a salary around $10,000, significantly better than what other entry-level jobs were paying. So I thought, *I like this. I'm pretty good at it, so I'll do this for a while.* I figured one day I'd go find a real job where I'd put on a tie every day and sit at a desk.

In 1976, when I was twenty-three, I was promoted to restaurant manager, a big deal for me. I managed one location for about ten months, then they moved me to the restaurant where I had started on crew. That was interesting because a lot of the people who worked there when I was getting started were still there. Now I was coming back in as their manager. That whole dynamic of managing your former peers was quite a learning experience.

My job became very competitive after the owner/operator sold out to the company. All the managers of the company-owned restaurants were vying to have the best sales. I did well enough that when I was twenty-five I became an area supervisor over four to five restaurants.

I never got the bug to own a restaurant because I worked for the company, and they were always developing me for the next position. That's a tradition that I have embraced, making sure we are always developing our people and keeping them moving up the ladder. I call it a "people pump," always creating the next generation of leaders.

The company had its struggles in the late 1990s and early 2000s when our stock took a hit. There was a perception that McDonald's growth was slowing It was thought that the way to address the problem was to diversify, buying some up-and-coming restaurant chains. The strategy was to broaden the portfolio but keep McDonald's as the main business. That's when we bought Chipotle, a pizza place out of Ohio called Donatos, and Boston Market, with the idea to nurture and bring along these younger companies. We learned, however, that a one-point increase in McDonald's sales from a profit standpoint was worth more than all those other brands combined. We ended up divesting those properties.

Chipotle turned out to be a big success so it could be argued that we shouldn't have sold it. But we've had a great run since then, after we refocused on the McDonald's business. Nobody can second-guess that decision.

One of the interesting things about our business is that it's been growing so well in spite of the fact that so many people don't want to admit that they eat at McDonald's. During my last two years in the West Division, I've seen the best results I can ever remember. There are plenty of people eating at McDonald's even if they may not say so. There's quite a dichotomy between what we're actually doing and the public perception.

I've been in my current position for eight years now, the longest I've ever held any job in McDonald's, and it's rewarding. It's hard work and I travel all the time, but the things I enjoyed when I was running a restaurant are the same things I enjoy today: working with my team, developing people, being able to orchestrate results. I'm just doing it at a different level.

McDonald's remains a dynamic work environment. For example, we're developing improvements in our restaurant management structure. Since 1955 we have had much the same system—a manager, a first assistant, a second assistant, and then hourly or swing managers. We're trying to do something more conducive to managing some of the higher-volume restaurants and it's exciting.

I did a lot of different jobs to get where I am today, and that's what people like about working here. You get opportunities to do things you never would in another company. I've worked on product development, managed real estate development, and supervised finance, even though I don't know a lick about finance.

Parents and young people should know that the same opportunities that existed back in 1969 exist in our restaurants today. We're still growing, we're trying to become more contemporary, and we're just as vital and vibrant today as we were fifty years ago.

DID YOU KNOW?

1969: Apollo 11 lands on the moon. Neil Armstrong and Buzz Aldrin walk on the moon.
The first automatic teller machine is installed in the US.

1970s

Drew Nieporent

AUTHOR'S NOTE

Most of the people whose stories are collected here initially worked at McDonald's with no agenda other than to earn an honest dollar for an honest day's work. Drew Nieporent had a very specific agenda. He was interested in the restaurant business at a young age and wanted to see how a McDonald's worked. He went on to become a restaurant impresario, founding a group of three dozen high-end restaurants around the world, including New York's Tribeca Grill, which he co-owns with actor Robert De Niro.

Seeing McDonald's on the resumes of applicants would be a huge plus.

My father was an attorney with the New York State Liquor Authority, which licensed restaurants, so my family regularly dined at many of the best restaurants in the city. TV was a novelty and always on in our house, and I remember watching Julia Child and the Galloping Gourmet. Cooking looked like an interesting way to make a living.

Even as a kid, I was aware of Ray Kroc's story and found it fascinating. Ray was a visionary—the McDonald brothers created this thing, but he was the man who took it to the next level. I wanted the experience of working in one of the restaurants. In the seventies, there were few McDonald's in New York City, so when one opened a block from where I lived, it felt like it was meant to be.

It was extraordinary to see how everything was thought out—from the toasting of the buns to handing the food to the customer, every little thing was thought out. I loved the efficiency, that you didn't have to wait a long time to get a hamburger. Some elements of the system I learned there I still use today.

McDonald's taught good crew camaraderie. I worked with people from different social and economic classes and had a great time, with never a dull moment. I picked up on things quickly and didn't make many mistakes, but once when I was training, I accidentally dropped a block of American cheese for the fish sandwiches in the fryer.

The managers were all funny guys with a good sense of humor, but they were tough on us. Nobody was a specialist. I thought what I was doing put me firmly in the realm of Quarter Pounder grill man, a position of respect. I could cook a thousand dollars' worth of food in an hour, yet they'd put me on a ladder to clean the ceiling. Nobody was a superstar.

Even though I earned minimum wage, it felt great to get a paycheck. It made me feel secure. Another lesson I remember is the McDonald's mantra—QSC, which stands for quality, service, and cleanliness. It's been forty years since I worked there, and QSC still sticks with me. In all my operations, it's elemental. You offer a quality product with great service in a scrupulously clean environment. It's terrific advice for any restaurant.

I went to Cornell Hotel School in the fall of 1973, so I was with McDonald's for about a year. They talked about McDonald's at Cornell, and one of the graduates went to work at McDonald's. He came back on a Friday afternoon, when alums would visit and give lectures to an auditorium full of students, and told us about his experience.

I know how to cook, but I chose to work in the front of the house versus the back, so I was a restaurateur from the beginning. The first restaurant I put my money into and owned was Montrachet, which opened in 1985. The chef was David Bouley, who has become very famous in his own right. We got three stars from the *New York Times*.

That attracted Robert De Niro, and the second restaurant, Tribeca Grill, opened five years later. That one is still there twenty-two years later. A few years after that, we launched the Japanese restaurant Nobu, which has gone on to open numerous other locations around the world. In 2008, we relaunched Montrachet as Corton, which received two Michelin Stars. In the last twenty-six years, I've opened thirty-six restaurants across the country and around the world.

My most recent project has taken me back to hamburgers—a hamburger concession in Madison Square Garden. I created The Daily Burger, and it's a phenomenal product. The burgers are outselling every other sandwich in the Garden. Before they added The Daily Burger to the menu, they were only selling about eighty hamburgers a day. Now they sell well over a thousand. Obviously, my approach was helped along by my experience with McDonald's.

As a current restaurant owner looking at applicants for jobs, seeing McDonald's on the resumes of applicants would be a huge plus. Maybe someone who's never worked at McDonald's would look at it differently and not see the benefit of having that experience, but the lessons I learned at McDonald's were invaluable to my career.

DID YOU KNOW?

McDonald's became a billion-dollar corporation
on December 17, 1972.

Andrew Dornenburg

AUTHOR'S NOTE

What can you learn flipping burgers that would be useful in an award-winning gourmet restaurant? Andrew Dornenburg says he learned a lot about teamwork and how to manage people under stressful conditions. In addition to being a noted chef, he's written a number of popular books including his best-selling *Becoming a Chef,* winner of the James Beard Book Award, and *Dining Out.*

It may have been Filet-O-Fish and fries at the time, but when it became filet mignon and roasted garlic mashed potatoes, the lesson was the same: it had to be hot, and it had to represent your best effort.

Once I'd outgrown my paper route, McDonald's was one of the few real jobs available to teenagers. With a work permit from school, I started when I was fifteen.

I was impressed with how seriously everyone took their work. They cared very much and took a lot of pride in what they did. It was not just slinging burgers. It was putting out a product that you yourself would eat—which we all did on our breaks—and would be proud to serve to others.

I first noticed the culture of McDonald's by working a week of morning shifts. The morning crew knew their regulars by name, order, and coffee preference. This was not just a faceless fast-food place on a stretch of a four-lane road in a bland California suburb; it was a community with real-life exchanges of people laughing, joking, and being fed, literally and figuratively.

The most challenging aspect of the job was keeping up! I could do yard work or deliver newspapers at my own pace, but the work at McDonald's was fast and demanding. When a rush hit, if you were the weak link on milkshakes (which were still done on spindles and flavored to order), everyone was affected. Despite all the systems, you still had to have eye-hand coordination, be organized, work fast, know what was ordered from whom, and make it correctly.

1972
Electronic mail is introduced.
First video arcade game Pong debuts.

The most fun and rewarding experience was definitely working the grill. In the seventies you worked a large flat-top grill like you see in diners. It was real cooking with sizzling burgers and the big tin salt and pepper shakers on the side of the grill. The grill was the engine that drove the restaurant.

On Saturdays and Sundays, I filled in for the groundskeeper who was off on weekends. It was very unglamorous work that started around 6:00 a.m., but the pay was great for a sixteen-year-old because what other teenager wanted to work that early on Saturday and Sunday? One day I accidentally washed the tile sidewalk that went all around the restaurant with the wrong cleaner, which turned white and powdery when it dried.

Another older coworker whom I really respected and looked up to had to re-do the job as I'd already left for the day by the time my error was discovered. When I found out about that, I felt terrible, but he just smiled and shrugged off what must have been a good half hour of hard mopping. Now that's teamwork.

When I first started at McDonald's, learning to be fast was a real issue. I wasn't naturally the quickest at doing new tasks, and my manager questioned whether I was cut out for the quick pace. I still have the memory of a manager stepping in to help me out in the French fry station, saying, "That's how you keep up!" It stung at the time, but he got his point across. However, in time, I did pick up significant speed.

When I look back on my work in the kitchens of top restaurants  in New York and Boston, I recall how much a slow or disorganized team member could affect everything—and make you question their career choice. More than once in the heat of kitchen service, I have had to ask a slow worker to step off the line and take over what he or she was doing.

I have never once told someone to keep up. Instead, I learned the phrase "Work with a sense of urgency," which is kinder and still gets the point across. I have jumped in to help any person in the restaurant who needed it because the work is very demanding, and it is easy to fall behind. You take a plate from a waiter, help the dishwasher, or hand fellow cooks ingredients they are low on—it's all in a day's work. I taught young cooks to draw a diagram of their cooking station to help them be more organized and visualize the steps of what they would be cooking before it hit the fire.

When I became a professional cook, I realized how much muscle memory I retained from that first job—to be on time, to work fast, work clean, have fun with the crew, and take pride in your work. It may have been Filet-O-Fish and fries at the time, but when it became filet mignon and roasted garlic mashed potatoes, the lesson was the same: It had to be hot, and it had to represent your best effort.

At every top-rated restaurant around the world, success is based on teamwork. Even the best cooks need servers, and servers need someone to pour their drinks and clean their tables. It is no different at McDonald's. I worked with a team that pulled for each other—the managers and all the crew always wanted each person on the team to succeed. It sounds corny, but it was true. The restaurant was very democratic and all the positions were looked at with the same amount of respect, from the cash register to the fry station. If you weren't strong in one position, they would help you find the position where you were most successful.

DID YOU KNOW?

1974: First Ronald McDonald House opened in Philadelphia, Pennsylvania.

HIRED 1974

Andie MacDowell

AUTHOR'S NOTE

One of the things about McDonald's that people rarely hear of is that many franchisees have given people down on their luck a chance to get back on their feet. Sometimes it works, and sometimes, as in the case of Andie MacDowell's mother, it doesn't. But life has a way of presenting opportunities where there is a crisis, and Andie made the most of her high school experience at McDonald's. Hers is a story that is both sad and inspiring, and in our interview Andie made it clear that she was comfortable sharing it.

Working at McDonald's was my independence. I loved the freedom of not having to ask anybody for money, of being able to take care of myself.

A s many children of alcoholics will tell you, I had to take on some adult responsibilities at an early age, and that's what brought me to McDonald's. My mother worked at a restaurant in my home town of Gaffney, South Carolina. After she'd gotten one too many DUIs she lost her driver's license, so I had to drive her to work and pick her up at the end of her shift.

I had worked one summer as a lifeguard, and when I was sixteen, it made sense for me to work with her at McDonald's since I was going there every day anyway. My mother and I were very compatible. We had a nice relationship, so it was sweet, actually.

My mother's disease was a big factor in how poor we were. Our heat used to get turned off, but my mother refused to take welfare. She had been a music teacher by profession and played the organ at church. But it became increasingly hard for her to keep jobs.

My friends and family were happy when I started working at the restaurant. Everybody came to visit, and I got free food, so it was a good situation. Knowing poverty, I found it so sad that at the end of the day we had to throw out the leftover food. It bothered me so much that some nights I'd secretly rescue the burgers from the dumpster and take them home for my dog.

1974

Leonardo Dicaprio and Jimmy Fallon born.

The whole time I worked there I never cooked. They always had me on the register, which I enjoyed. One of the things I remember being proud of was my ability to count back change. Today, the registers do the calculations, but back then I did it all day long. For eight hours in a row I counted change. Then when I went to sleep, I'd dream about counting change. It was exhausting.

It was a great environment to work in, with lots of camaraderie and teamwork. This is something that I've enjoyed in my career, working with a diverse group of people on projects.

In those days they'd let me work right up to closing on school nights, and I often did. Back then, in rural communities like ours, kids were allowed to drive quite young because they were needed to help out on the farms. People were also used to letting kids work late hours. In the summertime, I could work whenever I wanted. I was a hard worker and enjoyed having my own money, so I took all the hours McDonald's would give me.

Coming from my background, it was a big deal to be able to buy my own clothes. I'm a very independent person and working at McDonald's was my independence. I loved the freedom of not having to ask anybody for money, of being able to take care of myself. It was a crucial lesson for me to discover how highly I valued my independence.

The sad part of the story is that my mother loved working at McDonald's, but she got fired. One day she was really too drunk to work and should have called in sick. I made her some coffee and drove us to the restaurant, a decision I regretted later. There was a new manager on duty. When the assistant manager reported that my mother was intoxicated, the new manager fired her. That was devastating for us both.

I went in the next day and asked if she could get her job back. They  said they couldn't, so I quit. I couldn't go back to work there. It was just too sad. It was one of my toughest life experiences and not beautiful, but I'm comfortable sharing it.

Years later I had a chance to talk to the guy who had been the assistant manager. He told me he'd had no idea that reporting my mother to the new manager would get her fired. I didn't blame him or have hard feelings, but it upset him so much he cried.

McDonald's was my mother's last job. After she was fired, I did an intervention and tried to get her to go into a place to get sober, but it didn't work. One of the doctors at the state hospital said she would be dead in five years if I didn't get her committed. I didn't have the guts to do that. He turned out to be right. She died five years later of a heart attack. She did live long enough, though, to see me successful in my career and was very proud.

After McDonald's, I went off to college where I worked in the cafeteria. I had already learned good work ethics and was very dependable. In the summer I went down to the beach and worked at Pizza Hut. I also worked at the clothing store, Casual Corner, and as a cocktail waitress.

I saved my money and finally, with $2,000, I left Gaffney for New

York, never looked back, and my career took off. No one ever gave me another penny. Although I've had the opportunity to experience great wealth, I know that if it was all taken away from me, I would still be happy. I know what it's like to live on very little.

In spite of my mother losing her job, I've always had a lot of affection for what McDonald's does and what it represents. I've done things with Ronald McDonald House and my relationship with the company has always been good. I'm sure my mother is smiling, glad to see how well I have done.

DID YOU KNOW?

1974: Stephen King published his novel Carrie.

Ana Madan

One of my biggest challenges is keeping alive in my children the family tradition of working as hard as you can to take advantage of the opportunity we have had.

Work was always a group activity in my family. When I was about five years old, my parents, my brother, and I would get up before dawn, pile into my father's old Nash Rambler with a steering wheel that kept coming loose, and deliver directories for the telephone company. My fifteen-year-old brother would run up and put the phone books on people's porches, occasionally being chased by a dog. That was in Toms River, New Jersey, about an hour south of New York.

My parents had been professionals in Cuba. My mother had a doctorate in math and my dad had a degree in chemical engineering. He had also been a star athlete, winning both a gold and a silver medal in the 1955 Pan American Olympics in squash. When we got to the States, they had to start over and take what employment they could find. For a while they worked on an assembly line in a pill-bottling factory in Philadelphia.

My parents planned to get jobs teaching Spanish in the public schools, but first they had to learn English and become certified. My parents were working toward their master's degrees at Rutgers University when we delivered the phone books. They worked multiple jobs, five days a week, five nights a week, and studied in between.

While my parents and grandparents worked to master English, I helped them by acting as a translator. When I was about seven, we went to a department store to buy a television. The salesman patiently demonstrated for my parents how to operate the set. He began by holding up the plug and saying, "Now, when you get home, you plug this into the wall like so."

When I repeated it in Spanish, my dad made a face. "What does he think, that we didn't have television in Cuba?"

Outside of my home environment, I grew up living the American life, speaking English and doing the same things that American school kids did. At home we spoke only Spanish, ate Cuban food, and listened to Cuban music. My parents wanted us to know who we were and where we came from. That included making sure my brother and I appreciated that we had all escaped a terrible fate.

I was born in Cuba in 1960, in the middle of a purge of anti-communists and business people. My father, who had known Castro personally, was in prison with a forty-year sentence accused of supporting the counter-revolutionary movement. My grandparents and my brother had managed to get to America first. When I was five months old, in September 1960, my mother and I were able to fly from Havana to Miami. My father was also able to get to the United States, and our family reunited in Miami.

I was about eleven years old when I realized that Fidel Castro was a man. If he came on the television, my parents would turn it off, so I had no exposure. I would have nightmares about my brother, my parents, and me jumping rooftops with the Abominable Snowman chasing us. It took a long time to process all that.

As much as my parents wanted me to know my cultural roots, it was equally important that we become American citizens. It required taking a test in English. At nine years old, I tutored and quizzed my parents and grandparents. Everybody passed, and one day we went to the courthouse and proudly swore the oath with our hands over our hearts. I remember getting red, white, and blue carnations. It was a big deal in our family, a point of great pride.

My father always had an entrepreneurial spirit, and often talked about the time he and my mother happened to walk into a McDonald's in Miami shortly after their arrival here. He told her, "It would be nice to have one of these one day." My parents harbored that dream and saved their money for two decades, finally buying their first franchise in the early 1980s in New York.

Like the phone books, the restaurant became a family affair. Oftentimes a franchisee was someone who had already had success in another business. In our restaurant, family was the core of the crew. My father continued to teach school in the beginning just in case.

Our family opened our first restaurant on the corner of Fulton and Pearl Streets in Manhattan. This was before the South Street Seaport area was developed as a major tourist destination. In those days, there was nothing much in that district except a big fish market and the people who worked on and around Wall Street. We made our money at lunchtime.

My weekends were all spent at that restaurant. We had an apartment in the city where my father would stay during the week and where the rest of the family would stay when we worked the weekend shifts.

My first responsibility was making Happy Meal boxes. I spent a lot of time doing that. I also spent hours making shakes on the Multimixer. At the end of the day my arm was dotted with dried shake mix. There was always a lot of cleaning to be done. We were so meticulous we used toothbrushes to clean the edges and seams on the seats and seat boards.

When I got back to school on Monday mornings, my classmates would talk about the movies they'd seen or the parties they'd attended, and I was reminded of how different my life was. I never saw it as a negative. Work in my family was a positive experience. My parents were always grateful for the opportunity they had, so I enjoyed it. But it was tiring.

When I went off to college in Washington, DC, I swore I'd do anything with my life but work at McDonald's. I was getting a degree in international relations at American University and wanted to be a foreign diplomat. When I came home for the summer, I still helped run the restaurant, but I was certain it wasn't going to be my career.

1974
The Sting wins best picture at Academy Awards.

My parents were able to pay for my education, but I had to earn money to pay for other things I needed. I worked in a retail shop in a mall in Washington, DC. One day, while on a break, I overheard a man behind me talking about a McDonald's coming to the mall. I thought, Hell, no! I am *not* working there.

The man was the owner/operator and he was interviewing a young woman, offering her twenty dollars an hour to do local marketing for his restaurant. In those days the minimum wage was about three dollars an hour, so my curiosity was piqued. I waited until he was done, then walked over and introduced myself.

"You need me," I said. "You don't need to pay that lady twenty dollars. I'll do it for fifteen." And there I was, in a McDonald's uniform again after I'd sworn I'd never go back! I worked weekends, helping train the crew and the son of the franchisee.

After graduation, I returned home and looked for work, but in the end I decided to go into the family business. It was calling me. As much as

I didn't want to be there, it was saying, "This is where you should be."

When the Seaport area began to be redeveloped, we lost our lease. That turned out to be a blessing because it resulted in our owning franchises closer to home in New Jersey. That's when I became an owner/operator, in 1986. Today, we are still in business as a family. My dad and I run our six restaurants as an organization. I own five and keep one in my dad's name so that he's an owner/operator, but we are equal partners. My brother has a restaurant in South Jersey.

With all the success our family has had, one of my biggest challenges is keeping alive in my children the family tradition of working as hard as you can to take advantage of the opportunity we have had in America.

My father is considered a pioneer within McDonald's because when he became a franchisee, there were only a handful of Hispanic owner/operators across the country. At the beginning, there were so few Hispanic and African-American franchisees that they were grouped together in one association. Later, when they separated, my father remained active and became president of the National McDonald's Hispanic Owner/Operators Association in 1988-89. I've followed in his footsteps as a founding member of the Women's Owner/Operators Association and am the only woman or Hispanic ever to be president of the New York owner/operators marketing cooperative.

My father was also instrumental in bringing to the New York area a scholarship program, HACER (Hispanic American Commitment to Educational Resources), for college-bound Latinos that is today part of the Ronald McDonald House Charities. In 2012, the twenty-fifth anniversary of the program, we'll give out $500,000 in scholarships in the New York area.

DID YOU KNOW?

In 1971, Henry Garcia became McDonald's first Hispanic owner/operator, in Los Angeles.

HIRED 1974

Ed Sanchez

AUTHOR'S NOTE

Some of the most dramatic personal stories in this collection are told by new Americans. Ed Sanchez was born just before Fidel Castro took power in Cuba in 1959. He arrived in Miami when he was eight with his mother, two sisters, and the clothes they were wearing—nothing more. His remarkable career took him all the way from crew member to corporate officer, overseeing the Canada and Latin America markets. Then he switched hats and became CEO of one of McDonald's major suppliers.

The day I came home with a bigger paycheck than my stepfather's, he changed his tune.
"Wow! You really can make a career out of this."

*B*efore we left Cuba, my mother explained to my two sisters and me that our lives were about to change. We were going to a new country where a person could make anything they wanted of themselves. It would not be easy, she said. "You will have to study hard and work hard."

I was eight years old and had lived most of my life in a family that was coping with terrible loss. My father had opposed Castro and for that he had been executed by firing squad. My grandfather's successful dairy farm had been expropriated by the new government.

In 1966, five years after my father died, we were allowed to emigrate. My last moments on Cuban soil were traumatic. At the airport some soldiers separated me from my mother, took me into a room, and I was basically strip-searched. We weren't allowed to take any family photos, personal possessions, or clothes beyond what we were wearing.

So we started from scratch in Miami, living with another family—nine of us in a two-bedroom apartment. People often say, "That must have been tough." But for a kid, it was fun. My cousins were there, and we had fun playing together. On hot summer nights we'd sneak a dip in the swimming pool at a nearby apartment complex.

My mother, who had never worked outside the home and didn't even know how to cook, worked two jobs—at a coffee bar and decorating cakes at a bakery. It was in that bakery that I earned my first dollar. When I was old enough, I went to work with her on Saturdays and hauled hundred-pound sacks of flour they used to make the cakes. I earned five dollars for the day and was happy as a lark.

When I was in high school, McDonald's became an "in" place in the Cuban community to get a job. It was new and considered cool. I applied when I was fifteen and was told, "You've got to wait a few more months." I would ride my bike over every day and check to see if my application had been processed and if there was a job opening.

Finally the day came when the person in charge said, "You got the job. Here's a uniform. Start tomorrow after school." That was in 1974, and the person I was working for, Martha Klein, was one of the first female owner/operators for McDonald's. She had been running the store since her husband, Al, passed away in 1969.

I worked a few hours a day during the week and, being an early riser, I was glad to work the first shift on the weekends, from five o'clock to one o'clock. If the one o'clock person was late or didn't want to work, I'd take that second shift and work until about 8:00 p.m. I started out cleaning the lobby, earning $1.25 an hour.

I took every shift I could get and soon my job interfered with practice for the basketball team I was on. After a few missed sessions, the coach gave me an ultimatum. "Look, you either play basketball or you work. Which one are you going to do?" I was the sixth man on the team and not really tall enough to compete. Education and work were the two most important things in my immigrant mindset, so since I wasn't getting paid to play basketball, I stuck with McDonald's.

It was hard work, and at the end of the day my legs would ache from standing for so many hours. But it didn't feel like hard work at the time. It was fun, and I was helping support the family. Except for a few dollars of spending money, my paycheck went into the family cookie jar.

1974
People magazine debuts, with Mia Farrow gracing the cover.

Interacting with all those customers and coworkers brought me out of my shell. I learned how to work with people from all sorts of different backgrounds. Many on the crew had full-time day jobs. One guy was a manager for the post office.

When I graduated from high school, I decided to study mechanical engineering and started taking classes at a community college while continuing to work. My mother had remarried when I was thirteen, and my stepdad, an executive with a construction company, was more like a buddy than a father. He was worried that I was shortchanging my future. "You're in college now. You're working too many hours and not paying enough attention to your classes. What are you going to do, work for McDonald's for the rest of your life?"

I wasn't sure what I was going to do for the rest of my life, but in the meantime I wasn't ready to give up McDonald's. I continued to juggle classes and work. When the owner/operator decided to retire, McDonald's Corporation became the operator and I became an employee of the corporation. I was promoted to manager, and it started to click for me that this could be a career. I had a company car and a nice salary and was still learning a lot.

In 1982 I was promoted again, to supervisor of a group of restaurants. I was twenty-four years old and losing interest in engineering. I switched to taking business classes that were more applicable to my work. The day I came home with a bigger paycheck than my stepfather's he changed his tune. "Wow! You really can make a career out of this."

One of my proudest experiences was when I was given a struggling location to manage. Sales were subpar and food costs were too high. I got the management team together and each person took responsibility for one aspect of the business. It only took us three months to get it humming, producing the results we wanted. This taught me that to be a good manager, I needed to communicate the goals clearly, make sure everybody had a role in achieving them, and set reasonable benchmarks we could reach that would keep everyone motivated.

My career continued to evolve, but when McDonald's offered me a chance to interview for the job of country manager for Spain in 1988, I wavered. I didn't know anybody there, and it was a long way from my family. My mother and stepfather sat me down and said, "Look, this is going to be hard on all of us, but this is a big opportunity for you. Go over there and do the interview. If they offer you the job, take it."

I spent five years as the country manager and then opened up Portugal. When I returned to the US, I was appointed regional vice president for Central Florida, and later president for Latin America and Canada, the position I held for the last eight years of my McDonald's career.

In December of 2003 I retired from McDonald's and bought into Lopez Foods in Oklahoma City, a major supplier to McDonald's of meat products. It is the nation's largest Hispanic-owned meat processing company. I went into partnership with John Lopez, who had been a McDonald's franchisee. We both came up through the system.

Today, I have two college-aged kids, and I tell them from time to time what my mother told me all those years ago just before we left Cuba: "You can be anything you want in this country, but you have to want it enough to study hard and work hard."

HIRED 1976

Leroy Chiao, PhD

AUTHOR'S NOTE

Long before he became an engineer, a scientist, and an astronaut, Dr. Leroy Chiao had an analytical appreciation for the well-thought-out system for cooking and serving food at his first job at a McDonald's in California. He went on to apply the skills he learned there and later to master three languages, earn several degrees, join NASA, and spend 229 days in space, thirty-six of which he was outside the space station. The same principles that make a successful restaurant crew apply in most any setting, he says, and certainly when flying a space mission.

There are a lot of experiences at McDonald's that are valuable to have at that young age and have translated into almost anything I've done.

B efore I was sixteen, I earned money mowing lawns around the neighborhood and doing other odd jobs. It was okay, but I wanted to do something else. As soon as I was old enough, I applied at the McDonald's in Walnut Creek, California, about ten miles from home.

My Chinese family was like most Asian families and communities, where education and work ethic are highly valued. From an early age, my parents impressed upon me that I needed to do my very best in school and get good grades. I needed to work hard to get somewhere in life.

It was a little surprising to me when the McDonald's manager hired me on the spot, handed me a uniform, and told me to come back the next week for training and work. It was my first attempt to get a job. A few weeks later, my friends were asking me about my new job and when I told them how easy it had been, they applied, too. But none got hired.

I never found out why I was hired so quickly, but working there proved to be a status symbol. Because the restaurant was several miles from our high school, my fellow students saw it as a big deal that I drove myself all the way out there for work. Since I was the only one of my school peers who worked there, the job was a feather in my cap.

When I started, several things impressed me. It was hard work, and I was busy the whole time. I couldn't just stand around. They started me out on the grill. It was hot laying down hamburger patties, and I had to become part of this well-oiled, efficient machine. I remember rotating through the different stations. I started on the grill, then went over to dressing hamburgers, then to toasting buns, and then to the fry station.

I was impressed by how they had optimized the operations, and this was something I appreciated later as an engineer. Everything arrived on time. The buns came out and were dressed, the meat was pulled off the grill, the cheese was put on it, the top layer of buns went on, and they all went up to the front to be boxed. The whole operation was very efficient. There was a lot of pressure not to mess up your part, because that would slow down the machine.

I got to be pretty good at all the stations. My favorite was the fry station because it was a self-contained unit. It was entirely up to me to make the decisions on when to put down another batch of fries based on what the crowd looked like or what time it was. They wanted enough fries made without there being any waste. When I was in charge of the whole station, I was able to keep it clean the way it was supposed to be. That gave me a feeling of independence and responsibility.

I was usually tired after a shift and felt like I really earned the money I was paid. Getting that paycheck made me feel very adult. There are a lot of experiences at McDonald's, some subtle and some not, that are valuable to have at that young age. My time there taught me the value of working hard and being part of a team, and those are skills that have translated into almost everything I've done. That's something young people learn in an environment like that—if you want to work as part of a team, you're going to have to learn how to get along, cooperate, and help each other.

I left McDonald's for a couple of reasons. It was a bit out of the way, and I found out that I could make more money working as a busboy in a restaurant closer to home. I also had some friends who were working at that restaurant. I worked at McDonald's for a little under a year, and my experience there was good preparation for my new job.

1976
NASA's Viking 1 lander touchs down safely on the surface of Mars.

In my work as an engineer, the lessons I learned at McDonald's—being part of a team, always thinking ahead—have all been applicable. As a pilot, one of the things you learn is to constantly look at your instruments and think about what's coming next. You're never just sitting there in the cockpit daydreaming. You always get as far ahead of the aircraft as you can to anticipate the next things that are coming down the pike. What I learned at McDonald's can be used in just about any kind of career.

DID YOU KNOW?

NASA began operations on October 1, 1958.

James Collins

AUTHOR'S NOTE

McDonald's went through a growth spurt in the 1970s right around the time that America's manufacturing base began to lose ground to foreign competition. James Collins grew up in Cleveland where he experienced that shift firsthand. Urged as a young man to get a good union job, he discovered the downside of factory work and found his calling in the McDonald's system. Today he is a corporate officer and still planning his next move. His journey was aided by mentors in the company who saw more in him than he saw in himself. He also credits networking with other African-American McDonald's employees to learn how to navigate a corporate world his parents and grandparents had never known.

Do good when no one else is watching because you never know where your blessings are going to come from.

The message my grandparents gave my siblings and me was that the best jobs in Cleveland were in manufacturing. Those were union jobs that in those days paid a high hourly wage and came with generous benefits. Both my grandparents worked in a steel mill for decades, and that had been their route to the middle class. They'd tell us, "Get your ninety days in, and then you've got Blue Cross Blue Shield."

McDonald's was not, in their view, a career.

My father had left us when I was three, and my mother had passed away when I was about six. Our grandparents inherited us and gave us an accelerated course in hard work and ethics. My grandmother would often say, "You guys have got to learn how to think for yourselves because we're not promised to you." She meant that they were older and nobody knew when their time would come. They wanted to make sure we were capable of taking care of ourselves. So we grew up with a bit more responsibility, and I think we matured a little faster than we might have if our parents had raised us.

I earned my first money helping my brother with his paper route. After I became serious about sports in high school, I got summer jobs. I worked for the City of Lorain in the paint and sign division and, later, worked at a small quick-service chain restaurant.

My last two years of high school I went to vocational school, and at the end of our junior year, we were expected to get a job as part of our senior year curriculum. I always liked fashion—suits and ties and all that good stuff—so I applied to work at an upscale menswear store. I went to the interview full of hope, but the feedback I got was devastating. I didn't get the job because I didn't look the interviewer in the eye and because my handshake was limp, a wet noodle. It was a painful learning experience.

I had a cousin who worked at a McDonald's as a second assistant, and he helped me get hired. I have always been competitive, so whatever someone taught me, I wanted to excel at it. They started me out dressing the burgers. My supervisor noticed I had mastered it pretty quickly and asked me what my next move was. I would later learn that always identifying your next move is integral to the McDonald's culture. It's about what you want to do. That kept me motivated.

I worked my way up to grill and began to take a leadership role. It was like being captain of a sports team and getting the players pumped. When I'd say, "Okay, it's time to settle down, let's go," people listened and we got work done.

My cousin said to me once, "With the way you pick up on things around here, you could move up into salaried management and make a pretty good career out of this." I dismissed the remark as teasing, saying, "Man, you've got to be kidding me."

One day an area supervisor who oversaw multiple restaurants paid us a visit and stood by the bun toaster watching me work. I was doing what I normally did, and doing it the best I could with a little flair. I was just having fun. When the evaluation came back, I had been singled out for praise.

In spite of all that, I left McDonald's after a couple of years at the urging of my grandparents to get a real job. I had since started a family, and they were convinced I'd never make enough money at McDonald's to take care of them.

My manager, who had encouraged me by always asking what I wanted to do next, told me I was making a huge mistake and was quite disappointed by my decision. She had been teaching me things that swing managers and second assistants do. She probably saw more in me than I could see in myself. I was more of a soldier than a general. I couldn't see the managerial path.

"James, what do you think you're going for right now? You'll make that ten times over here, and you'll have so much more opportunity to grow."

All I could hear were the voices of my grandparents saying, "Get out there and get that fifteen to twenty-dollar an hour job." So I got a job as a brake press operator for a company in the heating and cooling equipment business. Everything was great for a year and a half. I bought a new car and felt secure about my ability to be a good provider. Then I got laid off.

Next I went to another large company that made air conditioning units. I did that for five months, until they went out of business. Then I sold insurance for a year and met a lot of people who were getting laid off from factory jobs. The decline of America's manufacturing belt was in full swing.

Thinking McDonald's wouldn't take me back, I applied and was hired at a Wendy's, just across the street. I was up to restaurant manager in about a year and a half. I was noticed by some people from McDonald's and was offered a position at the highest-volume restaurant in the Cleveland region. When that happened, I thought about something my grandmother always used to say. "Do good when no one else is watching because you never know where your blessings are going to come from." I connected her advice, which I took to heart, with being observed by the folks from McDonald's. You never know who's watching.

The company encouraged us to take one day out of thirty to devote to our own development. My strategy was to ask around and identify the sharpest person at the next level above me. Then I'd spend one day a month with him or her. I wanted to make sure that I connected with the people who were doing their jobs the best.

When I became a restaurant manager, my grandparents started to understand that it was a real career. They said, "He's doing pretty good there." When I became an operations manager and was able to buy a new house, they were proud. They said, "Wow! We never would have thought."

My grandmother's admonition to "do good when no one else is watching" has served me well throughout my career. One of the examples I often cite is the role Jim Flaum played in my life. Jim became the company regional manager about six months after I first became a restaurant manager. At the time, I didn't know who he was. I thought he was just a customer who'd come into the restaurant sometimes twice a day. Little did I know he was watching me and would play a big role in my career.

Sometime later we became friends, and he approached me one day with a proposition. He wanted to show me how to dress like an executive. At the time you could say I dressed with a bit of dash: pin-striped, one-button suits with gray matching shoes.

Jim was very diplomatic about it. "James, let me show you where I buy my suits." He took me to Dillard's department store and explained how to get fitted for a suit and then advised me to wait to buy it when they had a sale.

"You should always have a 100 percent wool suit," he said. "I know people think that it's going to be hot in the summertime, but always wear a 100 percent wool suit, 100 percent cotton shirt, and 100 percent silk tie. And get your pants cuffed with a full break." Then, after he helped me pick out a suit, shirt, and tie, he said, "I'm giving you a bonus so you can pay for it." He really fixed me up nice.

Years later, when I had become an operations director in that region, I had an employee in human resources who wore suit jackets that were too small for his frame. One day I took him out to the same store where my limp handshake had kept me from being hired. I bought him two suits and some shirts. I hope that someday he will pay it forward for someone else.

One of the opportunities that helped me in my career with the company came in 1985 when I was invited to participate in the Black Employee Network, one of the first of many diversity groups that have formed over the years. African Americans from all over our region would come together, attend educational classes, and learn to navigate the system. Today, there's the McDonald's African American Council (MA2C). There are also groups for employees who are Hispanic, Asian, women, and working mothers. These diversity groups have grown and are very active and influential.

The Black Employee Network was an early version of MA2C, and it helped people like me, whose grandparents had no experience in the corporate world to share with us kids. The Black Employee Network helped me and many others understand that some of the things we went through had nothing to do with our ethnicity. It was just how business was done. It helped people like me become comfortable in what was then a new environment for minorities.

McDonald's USA went through a major reorganization in 2001 and went from having five national divisions to three. The restructuring left me uncertain of what I'd do next. One of the division presidents, Don Thompson, thought my leadership skills would make me a valuable addition to the Greater Southwest Region. I started as a vice president and rose through the ranks to eventually became the vice president and general manager of that same region.

My career has continued to evolve. In 2011 I became vice president and general manager of McDonald's Florida Region, overseeing the marketing, finance, operations, franchising, training, and human resources functions for a region of more than 800 restaurants with over $2 billion in annual sales.

And I'm still asking myself, "What's your next move?"

DID YOU KNOW?

1976: Apple Computer Company is formed by Steve Jobs and Steve Wozniak.

HIRED 1977

Rick Colón

AUTHOR'S NOTE

From growing up on the dangerous streets of the South Bronx in the 1970s to being one of the top officers of McDonald's USA, Rick Colón describes his career as a pinch-me experience. He expresses amazement at the opportunities he's had and the opportunities that others like him have enjoyed. His story illustrates what companies like McDonald's represented to inner-city communities at that time, and his career has tracked big changes in Hispanic culture. He even got to meet Ray Kroc, under most unusual circumstances.

The day I came home and told my father I got promoted to manager, he beamed with pride. "You've really made it. You're a success!"

When I was in high school in the 1970s, the economy was in bad shape, and gasoline was rationed. Many kids in my school in New Haven, Connecticut, were working at Burger King or the department stores downtown. These were coveted jobs, but McDonald's was seen as a particular beacon of opportunity. Even the people who worked at Burger King tried to get hired at McDonald's.

As soon as I was old enough, I applied at the McDonald's that was within walking distance of our home. When I didn't get a call back, I waited awhile and applied again, without success. The word was that you needed to know someone.

One day I was talking about it with a teacher, and he said he was good friends with the manager who ran the downtown New Haven restaurant. He called his friend and scheduled an interview for me the next day. He told me to wear a jacket and tie to school. Our Puerto Rican family had left a dangerous neighborhood in the Bronx to come to New Haven. It was heaven by comparison, but we were still poor. I told my teacher I didn't have a jacket or a tie. The next day he brought both to school for me to wear to my interview. I credit my career break to him, and we've been friends ever since.

The interview went well, and the restaurant manager hired me. I was on my way. Until then I had few friends outside of sports. As soon as I started working at McDonald's, it was like I had this new big family of friends and a job that everyone envied. The work was strenuous but doing it as a crew member made it fun.

When I first started I was amazed at how detailed the training was and how neat and organized they kept the restaurant. Everything was in its place; everything was clean. You were expected to always keep your work station spotless while also taking care of the customers. I loved it, and my wife credits McDonald's for turning me into a neat freak at home—everything in the tool shed, garage, and basement is in its place.

I started up front at the register, which in those days was unusual. Typically the guys started in the back on the grill, and the ladies started up front. I wanted to be closer to the customers and asked to work the front counter.

I enjoyed going out into the lobby area, where I could chat with people and fix any problems. I made many friends, and we did fun things together outside of work, like picnics and softball games. People became so attached to the crew and the restaurant that even after they went off to college, many would come back over Thanksgiving break and Christmas and during the summer. They would start calling the restaurant in March saying, "Hey, I'll be out of school in a couple of months. I just want to make sure you know I'm available for the summer."

My experience as an athlete helped me learn to lead at McDonald's. I already had been trained in the team concept: good communication, hard work, and covering for your teammates. When I look back at my career, I think a lot of my success has to do with learning the importance of putting the team first and how I was able to build on that.

During my first year at McDonald's, I had the good luck to meet Ray Kroc. He was friends with the owner/operator and showed up at our restaurant one day, creating quite a stir. He was chairman of the board for McDonald's after all. He looked around, spotted me, and asked where the mop was.

"I'll get it. What do you need, Mr. Kroc?"

"Someone spilled a soda out front and I want to mop it up."

I was horrified that he thought a man in his position was expected to do such a menial task.

"Oh, no, Mr. Kroc! I can do it!"

"No, no, no," he said. "Just bring me a mop, and I'll get it. You keep taking care of the customers." I remember that moment like it was this morning.

By the time I graduated from high school, McDonald's had become so much a part of my life that it was the dominant topic among the comments people wrote in my yearbook: "Someday you're going to own your own McDonald's." "Someday I could see you being president of McDonald's." And somebody wrote, "Hopefully you're not flipping burgers forever."

After graduation I was promoted to what was then called breakfast manager, working weekdays from 5:00 a.m. to 1:00 p.m. I was responsible for opening the restaurant with a crew of about four people. Back then our breakfast shifts weren't very busy. When I got that promotion, I had to pinch myself. There I was, seventeen years old with the responsibility of managing people who were mostly older than I—moms, housewives, and recent college grads. A year earlier, I didn't even own a tie!

By the age of twenty, I was married and an attempt at college wasn't working out. My dream job would have been in law enforcement, but instead I was promoted to restaurant manager, running a million-dollar business with assistant managers reporting to me and a crew of about fifty.

People have asked me, "How did you become a restaurant manager at twenty years old?" I'd like to think it was because I was the best person. My bosses had certainly been training me, although I didn't realize that's what they were up to. Probably the real reason was because the company was growing so fast they were willing to take a chance on promoting some of us sooner than they might have otherwise.

My dad had fallen in love with McDonald's right from the beginning and thought I should try to make it a career. The day I came home and told him I got promoted to manager, he beamed with pride. "You've really made it. You're a success!"

I still had the bug to be a police officer, so I applied to a few departments. The North Haven Police called me in for an interview, but I discovered that the starting annual salary was only $14,400. As a manager at McDonald's I was earning $20,000. With a family to support, my decision was easy, and ever since I've enjoyed my passion for crime solving vicariously through TV police dramas.

> **1976**
> Top movies: *Rocky, Taxi Driver, Network, All the President's Men*

The owner/operator I worked for eventually had twenty-five restaurants in the New Haven–Bridgeport–Hartford area, a big organization. I rose through the ranks to become his operations director, working for him for sixteen years, until he retired. Some of his restaurants went to other franchisees and others became McDonald's corporate owned. The management team had the opportunity to become franchisees, work for another franchisee, or go work for the company. I chose to work for the company.

That was in 1994. Today, thirty-four years after I first put on a paper McDonald's hat, I'm senior vice president for the East Division, covering about 5,200 restaurants from Maine to the Keys. Never did I think in 1994 that I would ever reach this level.

I have two adult sons, the youngest of which has followed in my footsteps. He has been with McDonald's for ten years and runs one of our company restaurants in Lakeland, Florida. He keeps me grounded. When we have dinner he tells me what's working and what's not working. Every so often, he'll look at me skeptically and say, "You didn't make this decision, did you?" To which I reply, "Depends. Do you like it or not?"

As a Puerto Rican who grew up in the 1970s, I'm often reminded of how far the Hispanic community has come. When I was a restaurant manager in Connecticut, I was the only Hispanic manager among the state's 160 restaurants. I was one of the very few Hispanics in the corporation in my early days. Today, when I speak to audiences, I look out and see five hundred Latinos and Latinas, which blows me away.

I have a real appreciation for the remarkable careers of people whose journeys have been especially challenging. I felt that appreciation when I reconnected recently with a young man in our organization whose family fled an oppressive regime in South America. He had been a pharmacist back home, but here he started out flipping burgers at McDonald's.

Today, he is an area supervisor of five restaurants doing about $15 million in annual sales, applying for his citizenship, and owner of three houses he has converted into rentals. I'm biased, but I ask myself where else but in America, during one of this country's worst economic times, could someone have such success?

When I first started working at McDonald's, my proud father would stop by periodically and ask the restaurant manager how I was doing. Today, at age eighty-two, he still regularly visits his local McDonald's and drops my name. Employees who work in that restaurant tease me about my dad, saying, "Our mystery shopper was here today checking things out." To this day, the only quick-service restaurant he's ever eaten at is McDonald's.

DID YOU KNOW?

1977: Ray Kroc celebrates his 75th birthday.
His book is published, titled *Grinding It Out*.

HIRED 1978

Danitra Barnett

AUTHOR'S NOTE

In April 2011, McDonald's held an event called National Hiring Day, during which some 50,000 people were projected to be recruited at some 14,000 restaurants across the country, all on one day. When it was over, 62,000 had been hired. The event was organized by Danitra Barnett, vice president of human resources for McDonald's USA. Her journey is remarkable. She started out flipping burgers in Detroit and worked her way up despite many obstacles. She had the courage to insist on following the path she felt was best even though others had charted another course for her.

I learned to hire people who are different from me, who have different skills, and yes, who are more intelligent than I am. I make better decisions as a result.

*O*ne of my odd jobs as a youngster was ironing clothes for my aunt. She had three sons, one of whom worked for McDonald's. My cousin took a lot of pride in how he looked, so I put military creases in his McDonald's uniform to make sure it looked sharp.

It took three bus rides to get to my aunt's house where I grew up in Detroit, and the last stop was across the street from the McDonald's where my cousin worked. I went inside to visit one day and the crew and manager were remarking on how crisp he always looked. The manager, Tom Stratton, offered me a job right there on the spot. I was sixteen. It was so exciting to get my own baby blue McDonald's uniform, which I kept ironed and crisp, too.

My mother, a seamstress, had divorced and was remarried. There were five children in the family, plus another she had with my stepfather. We were three girls and three boys, so folks often called us the Black Brady Bunch. McDonald's was a Friday night ritual for our family. When I started working there, my siblings were jealous, and every one of them ended up following in my footsteps. I was the only one that stayed with it, though. Now some of them wish they had, too.

I was fast at everything in the restaurant and a fast learner. Being dependable and responsible by showing up for my shift on time was important. I didn't want to be the one who caused other people to have to work harder because I was late. Catching those three buses, I couldn't run the risk that one of them might be running slow, so I always left for work early.

In addition to my career, I met my husband of over thirty-two years through McDonald's. He worked at another location and used to come over on occasion to pick up supplies. He claimed that he always came to my line because I was fast, but he admitted later, "I would have waited in your line no matter how long it took." Shortly after we met he was transferred to my restaurant and asked me out on a date. He eventually asked me to marry him—three times. My mother said I had to wait until I was eighteen, which we did.

Later, when I moved into management, I began to learn about balancing budgets and projecting sales and profits, things that children in an African-American family often didn't have opportunities to learn. You just didn't have exposure to many folks who were positive role models and could teach you those skills.

My mother used to send us to the bank or the grocery store to expose us to some of those things, and she insisted that I save half of any money I earned. But it wasn't until I worked for McDonald's that I began to really understand profit-and-loss statements, balancing budgets, saving, and not overspending. I carried some of those lessons into how I managed my household as a young wife and mother, and I still use them today.

After I advanced to becoming an area supervisor, overseeing multiple restaurants, I realized that leading and managing people was my biggest responsibility. I decided I wanted to focus my career on human resources. My husband and I had moved from Detroit to Grand Rapids, Michigan. It was a culture shock for us. Grand Rapids was largely a white community at that time and most of the owner/operators were white males.

When I expressed an interest in human resources, I was told, "No, you can't move over into human resources because you're one of our affirmative action candidates, and we really have this operations career path outlined for you." I had no idea that there was this plan set up for me without my knowledge.

My mother always told me, "Never accept no for an answer," so I stuck to my guns. Eventually, the regional vice president overrode several other levels of people to let me move into human resources. That was over twenty years ago. I love it and have not looked back.

I've had a lot of support from family, friends, and colleagues along the way, but one who was skeptical for a long time was my biological father. He couldn't imagine McDonald's offering any of his five children a viable career. He often ribbed me, saying, "Are you kidding? Are you still flipping burgers?" I would proudly retort, "Every chance I get!"

He owned a successful heating-ventilating-air conditioning company in San Francisco. His business had become so lucrative that at one point he asked my husband and me if we would consider operating some McDonald's franchises for him if he bought them. We turned him down, enjoying the irony.

We relocated several times with McDonald's, something that I could not have imagined as a little girl growing up in Detroit. We've lived in three different parts of southern California and are now in the Chicago area. Those were broadening experiences for all of us and gave our children the chance to learn about different people. This was important to me as an African American because most of my siblings and relatives were born and raised in Detroit, and that's where you were expected to stay your whole life. Moving around the country helped shape me by opening my mind and giving me new opportunities.

I learned early that it was critical to have mentors throughout my career. For example, I was coached about being a bit too candid and direct with my opinions. As one person put it, I needed to add a little sugar to my vinegar. My mentors would say, "You have a tone that says you've got this standard and the person you're talking to isn't meeting your expectations. Figure out how to say it in a way that will make people more receptive."

Early on, I tended to hire people who were like me. When I transitioned into human resources, I learned to hire people who are different from me, who have different skills, who bring diversity to the table, and yes, who are more intelligent than I am. I make better decisions and accomplish more as a result. Since that time, my teams have always been diverse.

After more than two decades in human resources, I had the opportunity to help lead a national rollout of an event that had been successful in our western division—hiring day. In 2011, the first National Hiring Day resulted in 62,000 people being hired to work in our 14,000-plus restaurants. The event was well received and earned the company a great deal of positive press.

I'm a tough cookie, but when I reached my current role, vice president of human resources with responsibility for all our US restaurants, I almost cried for the first time in my career. Everything I experienced and learned as a crew person, an assistant manager, a restaurant manager, a supervisor, and a human resources professional had led me to that moment when I had responsibility for shaping the culture of our restaurants. This career has been my pie in the sky—a dream come true for this little girl from Detroit who started out ironing her cousin's uniform.

HIRED 1978

Janice L. Fields

AUTHOR'S NOTE

It would be hard to imagine a career as remarkable as that of Jan Fields. Starting out on crew working at the front counter, she discovered her calling—making people happy—and began her rise through the ranks. Thirty-two years later, in January 2010, she was named president of McDonald's USA, overseeing about 14,000 restaurants employing more than 800,000 employees. Jan's journey has inspired many other women in the business world, and she has made it a point to mentor individuals along the way.

"The most wasted of all days is one without laughter."
—e.e. cummings

Had it not been for the kind words of a stranger, my career might have been quite different. A few simple words of encouragement at the end of my first, frustrating day on a new job taught me an important lesson and changed my destiny.

I was a twenty-two-year-old college student in Dayton, Ohio. A married mother of a little girl, I had no specific career path in mind. All I knew was that I needed a job to help pay my college expenses. On my way to interview for a position as an office assistant one day, I had some spare time and stopped at a McDonald's to get something to drink. I noticed a sign—Help Wanted, Flexible Hours—which sounded promising to a mother juggling school and family. I asked someone behind the counter what *flexible* meant and learned that I could work in the evenings, something the office job couldn't offer. Working nights was ideal because that's when my husband was home and able to take care of our daughter. I filled out the application and was hired pretty much on the spot.

My first shift on the job, I was assigned to make French fries. Who knew there were so many rules and procedures just for making fries? I felt so overwhelmed that I left my shift crying and resolved to find another job.

After I got home, the phone rang. It was one of my new coworkers from the restaurant. "Hey, I heard you did great today! I'm sorry to ask on short notice, but do you think you could help me out and cover my shift tomorrow?" I decided to give it a second chance the next evening. That Friday night, I was assigned to work the register at the front counter. Despite being naturally shy, I discovered that I loved talking with the customers.

I had a knack for reading faces and could tell if someone was happy or ready to complain. A person who had waited too long to be served and was wearing a frown inspired me to try to turn it into a smile. It felt great to be helping others, especially parents with kids. I had my own child so I could relate.

Had it not been for that phone call, I might never have discovered that I'm a people person. That taught me a big lesson: Don't quit over one person or one event. I learned that you had to give things a second try.

But not everyone was on board with my new job. My family expressed some skepticism at first. They were puzzled about why I had chosen to work at McDonald's and wondered how it could lead to a career for me.

The answer wasn't long in coming. I went from being a crew person to a swing manager within a couple of months. Then I moved up to second assistant manager, first assistant manager, and finally restaurant manager—all within my first year. Pretty quickly my family stopped worrying.

I spent two years managing a restaurant at a time when there were few women in that position. Of the forty restaurants in the Dayton market, only one other had a female manager. After that I was promoted to managing multiple restaurants, then went into higher management.

Back then, there was an infectious feeling of opportunity surrounding the brand. I was making a decent income and the company was growing, opening a lot of new restaurants. The decision to stay was easy because I was having fun. As long as I'm enjoying this, I thought, I'm sticking around. Three decades later, I'm still having fun and wake up every day happy to work for a company that is rich with opportunity.

Service, family, community, and *team* are words you hear constantly at McDonald's because we want everyone to know that they are valued. In order to run a successful restaurant, it's crucial that people feel they can depend on each other. A group of crew members can feel like a second family.

1978

Sony introduces the Walkman, the first portable stereo.

For me, being part of the McFamily has given me an opportunity to mentor others and teach them things I've learned along the way. I met one of my best friends when I was a field consultant advising franchisees. She was one of a handful of women managers and a very hard worker. But she lacked self-confidence and received little encouragement from her bosses, who were mostly men.

Our friendship began right after she had gotten a promotion. I noticed she was wearing socks instead of nylons. I took her shopping to buy the right clothes. From that moment on, she and I supported each other, listening to and coaching each other. Over the years, I have watched with pride as she achieved great success and have benefitted often from advice she's given me. The spirit of our friendship and the way it began is common within the McFamily. As one of our favorite Ray Kroc sayings goes, "None of us is as good as all of us."

As I learned when I was starting out, it's a lot more complicated to run a busy restaurant than it might look. It involves hard work, diligence, efficiency, common sense, and relationships—basic skills we teach young people. I truly believe that with the skills you learn at McDonald's, you can make it anywhere.

DID YOU KNOW?

1978: 25 billionth hamburger served

HIRED 1978

Carla Harris

AUTHOR'S NOTE

When I first heard Carla Harris speak at a McDonald's event, I was impressed with what she had to say and the energy and enthusiasm with which she said it. She credits the sales skills she developed working behind the counter as a young woman with helping her land a job on Wall Street. Today she is a managing director at Morgan Stanley, and in her spare time is a recording artist, motivational author, and speaker. She is a gospel singer who has performed at Carnegie Hall. Among the skills she said she learned on crew, listening to customers has been one of the most valuable.

There really is no such thing as a dead-end job.
It's what you take away from it that adds value.

When I was in eighth grade, Willard and Leenie Payne became the first African-American franchisees to open a McDonald's in Jacksonville, Florida, where I lived. It was all the rage at the time, and some of the older kids I knew got jobs there. I remember thinking that the uniforms were pretty cool.

The restaurant was at an ideal location, a busy intersection with no competition. Soon after, the Paynes opened a second restaurant in another African-American neighborhood, close to three hospitals. The Paynes were involved in the community, so I got to know them through our church, Saint Pius, and because their daughter attended my high school.

My parents were hard workers and my grandmother was an entrepreneur, so I grew up with a strong work ethic. My grandmother ran the neighborhood tavern for fifty years. I was good at math and I helped her with her bookkeeping from the time I was thirteen. But I thought a job at McDonald's would be an opportunity to have my own money and my own responsibility. By the time I was sixteen, I definitely wanted to work for the Paynes.

First, I had to sell my father. He agreed to let me apply on one condition: "If you have one grade, just one, that goes down, you're done with the job." Getting my first paycheck made me even more determined to keep my job, so I made sure to keep my grades up. I worked from 1978 through the summer of 1980, when I went off to college at Harvard, and worked there again the summer after my freshman year.

In the African-American community where I grew up, most parents pushed their children to do well in school. Growing up in the sixties and seventies, we all looked to education as the key to succeeding in the world, regardless of what you ended up doing. The general philosophy was that if you got a great education you could make life happen. If you didn't, life would happen to you.

My mother's philosophy was, "The world may not be fair, but if you want to make sure that you get yours, you must always be excellent." She knew unfair treatment by others was no excuse for subpar performance. "Go for the highest," she said. "If you want an A, go for the A plus. That way, if you get shaved a little bit, you'll still have your A." That philosophy has been behind much of my success.

McDonald's put everyone on a ninety-day probation before they were technically considered on board. We were told things like, "Serve your customers in sixty seconds" and "Always suggest a sale, like an order of fries to go with a Big Mac." I took all of it seriously and got crew member of the month while I was still on probation.

We were told that field consultants would come in unannounced to test whether we served them in sixty seconds, suggested a sale, or gave service with a smile. I assumed that anyone in line could be a field consultant, and I wanted to pass the test. This helped me learn to adapt quickly.

The things that make you successful on crew are things that make you successful in almost any career. I never knew who'd be standing at my register or what kind of attitude they'd have. It's the same in business: I never know if a client is going to be tough or easy, forthcoming or reticent. Adaptability is crucial. You have to quickly determine how to handle each situation appropriately. You need to know how to treat customers well and listen closely. Maybe when a customer walked in, he or she didn't think they wanted fries, but my job was to entice the customer into buying them as part of the order. A lot of this had to do with how I approached and served people.

> **1978**
>
> Ilinois Bell Company introduces first Cellular Mobile Phone System.

My mother's advice helped me in my McDonald's experience, and my McDonald's experience helped me sell myself while interviewing for my first Wall Street job. You might think the two jobs have nothing to do with each other. But in fact, the interviewer was looking for exactly those skills I had learned at McDonald's. What they valued was that I already knew how to deal with customers, be assertive in sales, penetrate the client's thoughts, and create a measure of respect among my peers—all of which I needed to be successful on Wall Street.

The biggest lesson I learned at McDonald's was managing upward. I'd only had my grandmother as a boss, so McDonald's was my first time dealing with a manager. I quickly learned that if I was dependable and had a good attitude, the manager was more willing to work with me. If I wanted a day off, I needed to be in good standing with the managers because they weren't obligated to grant me the request.

The foundation of building a good relationship with your colleagues is delivering what is asked of you. I call this "performance currency." The beauty is that it can be spent as needed to build a relationship, make special requests, or even when you need a second chance, because with performance currency in your bank, you have a reputation of being someone who performs and always delivers excellence.

I banked my performance currency from my first days at McDonald's when I was being trained. I learned to do everything well and also focused on being fast and accurate, collaborating with my coworkers, and providing friendly service. This created the currency I needed to have a great relationship with my bosses. People like me who had the most currency got first pick at opportunities to get extra hours.

The more seasoned I become in a client-oriented business, the more of a premium I put on great listening skills. By listening well, I figure out what people really mean, which can sometimes differ from what they say. This gives me a competitive edge.

I do quite a lot of public speaking and when I'm addressing younger audiences I mention my McDonald's experience to illustrate what great training it is. There can be a stigma among kids about McDonald's. They think, "I don't want to work at McDonald's. Who wants to flip hamburgers?" They don't realize that it could lead to a number of different opportunities, both inside and outside of the company.

I use stories about my McDonald's days to show my audiences that valuable lessons can be learned at any job. Thanks to my experience on crew, I learned early on that what matters most is understanding what the customers really want and how to sell it to them. There really is no such thing as a dead-end job. It's what you take away from it that adds value.

DID YOU KNOW?

1980: McDonald's marks its 25th anniversary.
Sundaes were added to the menu.

HIRED 1978

Leo Lopez

AUTHOR'S NOTE

It often surprises people to learn that McDonald's franchisees are independent businesspeople with strong entrepreneurial spirits and instincts. As the *Wall Street Journal* put it in an early 2012 front-page feature, the company's "secret sauce has always been its small-business franchisees." Leo Lopez, son of Cuban émigrés, worked for an entrepreneurial owner/operator in Miami from high school through college. He decided to pursue a career in banking, only to find himself lured back to become an owner/operator himself. Like many other franchisees, Leo has purchased, grown, and sold multiple locations and he has found an innovative way to reduce his facilities maintenance costs and down time by grooming his own experts in-house. For years, Leo has been involved with the McDonald's Hispanic Operators Association, an organization that keeps the company and its Hispanic owner/operators aligned to ensure success.

*My grandfather would often talk to me about America
and the opportunity it offered anyone who worked hard.*

A scratched windshield changed the course of my life. I was fifteen years old, working at a gas station on the edge of the Everglades near Miami. One weekend a mud-covered Jeep pulled in and the owner said, "Hey, kid, could you clean my windshield?"

I got the scraper and pressed down so hard that I gouged the windshield with the metal blade. The station owner had to pay for a replacement, and I was told they couldn't give me any more hours. So I applied at a McDonald's that was three blocks from my house. I could ride my bike there and work flexible hours around my class and busy sports schedules. My passion was basketball, but I also played baseball.

My friends thought it was great that I was working at McDonald's and a couple of them ended up working there too, as did my younger brother. I started out on the grill, and all I did the first month for four hours a day was make Quarter Pounders. It was the original open kitchen design, so customers could watch us work. The company placed great emphasis on everything being spotless. I remember little kids looking in at us through the windows and saying things like, "Wow! Look at all those hamburgers they're making so fast all at once."

When I turned seventeen, Ralph, an assistant managers who worked at that restaurant and had been a mentor to me, went to work for a new owner/operator in Miami and persuaded me to join him. Ralph was about four or five years older. He knew how to make a laborious job of making food all day and serving customers fun and challenging. He said things like, "I bet you can't make a hundred of those without making a mistake."

Ralph saw in me a willingness to always try to do things the right way. When somebody was doing something incorrectly, I tried to help. I quickly became a crew chief and would work with new hires to show them the ropes. I had already been told I had leadership potential in sports. Unlike the gas station, where I often worked alone, McDonald's gave me a chance to develop those skills.

I became a restaurant manager when I was twenty and continued to work through college, earning a degree in finance and international business. I wanted to work in the field I had studied so I left McDonald's in 1986 to take a job in banking as an entry-level financial analyst. I enjoyed banking and had no intention of going back to the restaurant business. But life throws you curve balls.

Angel Rodriguez was an owner/operator of one of the restaurants where I worked. I had been close to Angel and his father and mother. Angel was an accountant, so we were able to talk about the financial side of the business. I consider him one of the most important mentors in my life. His parents would come in and help us all clean the restaurants at the end of the three busiest days—Friday, Saturday, and Sunday. His parents were part of the crew family and treated us all well, and I became close with his father. When Angel's father died, I attended his funeral. At the funeral, two regional directors from McDonald's I knew from working with Angel encouraged me to consider being an owner/operator, saying, "We think you'd do well." They've both since left the company, but they planted the seed.

I had started with Angel right after he'd bought his first restaurant, a low-volume location that was losing money. Through perseverance and hard work, he had grown the business, and by the time of his dad's death, he had three good locations and was working on a fourth. His lifestyle and standard of living had improved dramatically, and his success was appealing to me. Being an owner/operator was a new idea, and it got me thinking.

My parents and grandparents fled Fidel Castro's Cuba in the early 1960s. They first went to Spain, where my brother and I were born, then immigrated to the US. We lived in New York and then settled in Miami. I grew up in a culture of fiercely entrepreneurial expatriates. My grandfather had been a businessman and a federal legislator in Cuba. He lived until I was twenty and would often talk to me about America and the opportunity it offered anyone who wanted to work hard. He said, "I'm too old to take advantage of that, but you certainly can."

So I bought my first McDonald's in 1989 when I was twenty-six. My family and I moved from Miami to Orlando, where the restaurant was located. I asked my brother, Eddie, who was then driving tractor-trailers, to move to Orlando and work for me. Eddie had worked with me at McDonald's for several years, but his interests had taken him elsewhere. Now we were back together under the Golden Arches.

While he worked with me, Eddie also became a paramedic, eventually working full time at that while he was helping me. His strongest skill set was working with his hands, fixing things around the restaurant. As soon as I had the opportunity, I said, "Eddie, why don't you let me put you through refrigeration school?" So he went to different trade schools while he was working. He enjoyed the work and became my in-house equipment expert as I purchased additional restaurants.

Franchisees often swap resources and when owner/operators asked who we used to do our air-conditioning, I told them, "I use my brother. He's really good." In time, Eddie got so many customers he started his own business, and today he services many of the McDonald's restaurants in the Orlando area. Our grandfather would have been proud of us both.

About five years ago, we sold our restaurants in Orlando and came back home to Miami. My wife, Cindy, was recently approved as an owner/operator, and now we own nine restaurants, which would provide plenty of work for Eddie if he were closer. Instead, we have two in-house maintenance folks, and there's always something to do. We've sent both of them to classes, seminars, and training programs so they are fully certified and up to date on the latest technologies. My experience sending Eddie to school has paid off. Now by training my own maintenance workers, I've greatly reduced my expenses and down time.

My father knew the owner of the gas station out by the Everglades where a scratched windshield altered my life's course. When I had become an established owner/operator of multiple restaurants, my father paid a visit and joked with the owner's son, "It's a good thing your father got rid of Leo. Just imagine how many gas stations he might have owned!"

I'm glad I chose to follow my grandfather's advice and became a successful entrepreneur. Owning my own business has meant a great deal of hard work, but to me, McDonald's has always equaled opportunity.

Ajay K. Patel

AUTHOR'S NOTE

Imagine being plucked out of the world you know today and dropped into the middle of Mumbai, India, not knowing the language and living on a student's budget. That's about what Ajay Patel experienced coming to America from Mumbai at the age of eighteen. He looked and felt out of place, was bewildered by culture shock, and wanted to go home. Two people reached out to him just when he needed it—a neighbor and later the manager of a McDonald's. Today, he is an owner/operator in Louisiana with an only-in-America story to tell.

The culture of the company and the attitude of America is that where you came from doesn't define who you are.

B ecoming an American was a fluke. My family never intended me to come to America at all. It happened because I was the last member of my immediate family still living in India. My mother had died in Mumbai when I was fifteen. My sister was living in New Jersey.

My father had been a chemical salesman but had gone to the States to help my brother get his citizenship papers. The process was taking longer than expected, and my father had been away almost two years.

My father was living with my brother, who was about to graduate from Oklahoma State. Then they planned to move to Louisiana where my brother's first job awaited. The family was scattered.

So my father decided, "Let's just bring Ajay here and see what happens."

What happened was that I—who grew up in the tropics—landed in New York in early 1977 without a coat, in the middle of one of the worst winters in history. I stayed with an uncle on Long Island while learning English and dreamed of home. The vision of America I had before—Elvis, sunlight on rolling farmland, everybody wealthy—was replaced by my new reality: a land where the sun never shone, the ice never melted, and foreigners were just barely tolerated.

Every weekday I trudged through chest-high snow for about half a mile to get to the first of three buses that took me to school and back. Then a stranger reached out.

Roger lived nearby and drove a Corvette. One day, as I was climbing over a hill of snow, he stopped and rolled down his window. "You know what? I work right near your school. If you want to go early, I'll take you and bring you back when you get done." The rest of that winter he picked me up and brought me back home many times. That was my first experience with the genuine America, where strangers open their hearts and help others. I often think about Roger to this day.

When spring finally arrived, I finished my high school requirements and English lessons and joined my father and brother in Lafayette, Louisiana. We were a family of bachelors.

A relative had helped me pay my school fees that winter, but I was going to have to come up with the money by August for my first semester at the University of Southwestern Louisiana in Lafayette. My dad said, "Your brother is just starting out, and I don't have anything. So you're going to have to work to pay your tuition."

So off I went, walking down the main commercial street in Lafayette, stopping in every quick-service restaurant there was. In my broken

English, I asked if they were hiring and filled out the applications that I was assured would be kept on file. I looked so different and my language skills were so rough that I knew I'd never get a call back.

I had been in eight or nine businesses and was becoming discouraged when I hit McDonald's. I handed my application to someone who took it immediately to the back and handed it to the manager. He was sitting behind a half wall. I watched him scan the page and then lean back in his chair to get a better look at me. He nodded.

"Okay, he wants to talk to you."

The manager came out from behind the counter and spoke with me for a quite a while.

Finally, he said, "You don't speak very much English, do you?"

"Yeah, I know," I said, bracing for rejection.

"Suppose we put you in the back. Can you cook?"

I'd made an omelet once or twice, but that was it.

"Sure!"

"Okay, son. You've got yourself a job."

I practically ran all the way home and burst in shouting, "Dad, I got a job!" I had no idea what I wanted to do with my life. All I knew was that my family insisted I earn a college degree and now I would have the money to get started.

Up until my first day at McDonald's, I'd been isolated from strangers by culture and language differences. Suddenly I had become part of a whole family unit. Everyone was welcoming. No one made me feel like an outsider. I was treated the same as everyone else.

Early on I discovered that when people wanted to take time off for a date or a concert, it was hard to find someone to cover their shifts. With no social life to interfere and tuition looming, I became the go-to guy for covering shifts. I loved being busy and making money, and it enhanced my reputation. The big break came when Don, the coolest dude in the restaurant and the guy all the girls liked, took me under his wing. He worked on the grill as well and began looking out for me, keeping me from making too many foolish mistakes. I wasn't cool, but it was cool having him for a friend.

A couple of months into my job, language was still a problem. Most of my coworkers were teenagers who had their own slang and regionalisms. I couldn't understand it all, so I made mistakes. Sometimes I produced more or less food than they had requested.

One day the manager took me in the back and said, "Unless you get a handle on this language barrier, I'm going to have to let you go." I went back to work worried, and it must have showed. Don said, "Don't worry about it, man. We'll take care of it." He started teaching me the slang I needed to catch up, and my job was saved.

When school started, I continued to work and continued to rack up the hours. But when I started bringing home Bs, Cs, and then a couple of Ds, my dad put his foot down. "Okay, from now on your brother will pay the tuition. You need to quit working and pay attention to your grades."

There was no way I was giving up what I had at McDonald's. My English was rapidly improving, I was starting to get promotions, and I had a social life. My dad issued an ultimatum: if my grades didn't improve, I'd have to quit my job. So I worked harder on my studies, raised my grades, and was allowed to keep my job. It was a tough balancing act. I worked so much that it took me six years to earn my degree.

When I did finally graduate with a business management degree in 1984, I took three months of vacation to visit India and returned to a new position as a restaurant manager in the States. I married my wife, Bindu, in 1986. My entrepreneurial father-in-law suggested, "Why don't you become a franchisee? There's nothing like owning your own business." I thought about it, but was hesitant because of the big financial investment involved. It was Bindu's persistence that convinced me.

She believed I could do it, and every day she asked me, "Have you decided about becoming a franchisee? I think it's a good idea. You should do it." I finally bought my first franchise in 1992. Now I have seven restaurants in rural towns in southwest Louisiana and two of my three sons hope to become franchisees one day.

My proudest accomplishment is having been elected twice by all the franchisees in our seven-state region to represent them on the National Leadership Council. That is the owner/operator's governing body that considers equipment, service systems, and profitability initiatives affecting all 14,000 restaurants. Considering how I began, this honor, more than any other recognition, illustrates what I like best about the culture of the company and the attitude of America: where you came from doesn't define who you are.

DID YOU KNOW?

McDonald's first opened in India in 1996. Its menu featured the Maharaja-Mac™, a sandwich made with lamb. Today the Maharaja-Mac™ is made with chicken.

HIRED 1978

Michael A. Smerconish

AUTHOR'S NOTE

One of the threads weaving itself through these stories is nostalgia for a work ethic that seems to have fallen out of favor. This has been a frequent topic for radio talk show host and MSNBC political commentator Michael Smerconish. He has spoken and written about his experiences working on crew at a restaurant in his hometown in suburban Philadelphia. Among his observations is the irony that McDonald's has to recruit help when so many young people are sitting at home out of work.

If I were in college admissions, I would have a lot more respect for a person who had punched a clock, gotten a little dirty, and learned how to rotate stock than someone who had a glamorous internship.

When I was young nobody could say that grass grew under my feet. I worked many different jobs when I was a kid. I delivered flowers, I delivered outdoor furniture, I painted address numbers on the curbs of thousands of homes one summer. I have always, for better or worse, been out there hustling.

My McDonald's job stands out because it was my introduction to an organizational atmosphere, where I had to be trained and had to punch a clock. I discovered what it was like to have taxes taken out of my paycheck. The job was much more structured than the others, and that was a benefit to me.

The restaurant in our town opened in 1977, during a recession. On day one there was a long line out the door of people who wanted to work there. My mom actually got in the line to see if I could get a job. I wasn't sixteen yet, so I had to wait until 1978. I went back, got hired, and worked there between one and two years. For the entire duration, I chose to work as a maintenance man.

I went through the training for the front counter and the grill and so on, but once that was done, I asked and was allowed to just do maintenance. I liked working in the early mornings, not having to wear a uniform, and being outdoors, plus the work appealed to my fastidious nature. I mopped floors, emptied trash cans, cleaned the bathrooms, washed the windows, and picked up trash in the parking lot.

The place was fun because a number of kids I went to school with also worked there, and we all got along. We had a softball team that played other McDonald's restaurants in the area. There was a cohesive feel to it, and I felt no condescension from anybody at school for working there. All my friends had jobs when we were that age.

One of my jobs was rotating the buns. When I brought up new buns from the storage basement, I had to carefully rearrange the rack so that the older buns were on top and used first. This way, none of the buns got stale. McDonald's was very strict about freshness. I never learned something like that anywhere else. Even today, I always reach for whatever container

1978

Gold reaches an all-time high of $200 per ounce

of milk is open in my fridge before opening a new one, because of my work restacking those buns.

Certain other things stand out in my mind as impressive. One day we got a phone tip from another restaurant that a McDonald's evaluation team had just made a surprise visit and was headed our way. There was a call to battle stations to ensure the place was shipshape. Then, sure enough, a big bus pulled into the driveway, and a group of managers piled out. They all got in line like customers and ordered different meals while holding stopwatches. It was intense, but I thought it spoke well for the company.

Today, I see a trend, particularly in the suburb where I live, that troubles me. Parents push their kids toward glamorous internships they think are going to look impressive on a college application or a future resume. If I were in college admissions or hiring someone, I would have a lot more respect for a person who had punched a clock, gotten a little dirty, learned how to rotate stock, and everything else a crew member does. There are a lot lessons you learn in a job like that.

The irony is that many of my neighbors who are parents did those sort of jobs when they were young, yet they seem to prefer that their kids stay home unemployed rather than work at McDonald's. This is a bigger issue. People who reach a higher rung on the social or economic ladder than their parents did tend to lose sight of the lessons that helped them be successful and neglect to pass those lessons on to their kids. As a parent, I try not to forget what afforded me the opportunity to have the choices I do and make sure that my kids are in touch with that. I would like my sons to have that kind of experience when they're old enough. I talk about my experiences with them, and I've taken them to see the restaurant where I worked.

Years after I worked at McDonald's, I read *McDonald's: Behind the Arches*, which was the back story of the McDonald brothers and Ray Kroc and how the chain was established. McDonald's is a great American success story, and I'm proud to have worked there.

HIRED 1979

Mindy Bloom

AUTHOR'S NOTE

Many crew members move up into the ranks of management, a few of those become owner/operators, and a small number become vendors. Mindy Bloom's journey is unique because it began when she was a child meeting Ronald McDonald, continued when she worked on crew, then later for a vendor, and came full circle when she became development director of the Ronald McDonald House in Winston-Salem, North Carolina. The powerful story she shares here about a little girl named Serena illustrates why so many are passionate about Ronald McDonald House Charities.

Just like working on crew at a restaurant, at the House it's a team effort. If you're walking down the hall and you see that somebody needs something, you pitch in.

*M*y first memory of McDonald's was meeting Ronald McDonald when I was about seven or eight years old. My mom was a big fan of the restaurants and when one opened near our house in Portsmouth, Virginia, she made sure we were there on opening day. With my sister and a family friend, we stood on line for what seemed like hours to hold Ronald's hand. What a thrill that was!

I grew up in a middle-class family with a strong work ethic. My father was a vice president for a waste disposal company, and my mother ran a business from home selling personalized gifts. I was eager to earn my own spending money, so I began as early as I could with odd jobs like babysitting. Later, my sister and I both worked as cashiers at a grocery store. One summer we vacationed in a bungalow at Virginia Beach, where I worked in a souvenir shop.

My official career began the summer of 1979, just before my senior year. I came home and told the family I'd gotten a job at McDonald's. My father said, "You made a good decision." How right he turned out to be!

Before I'd even stepped behind the counter, I learned my first lesson. I arrived at 5:45 in the evening, and my boss said, "At 5:45 you need to be *ready* to work, not putting your purse down, not putting your hat on." She only had to tell me once. I was glad to work there and would do nothing to jeopardize the opportunity.

It was good to get that lesson early because when I got to college, it inspired me to always show up for class on time. When I started my first full-time job, I made sure to be at my desk, ready to work, right on time.

Having worked in a grocery store and a souvenir shop, I already knew how to run a register and I was comfortable interacting with people, so that's where I started out at the restaurant. We had a group of loyal customers who I enjoyed getting to know. I also liked being cashier because I was one of the few who knew how to count back change aloud to customers. The regulars always commented, "You always count my change back. I like that." As basic as it sounds, counting change can be a challenge, especially during a lunch rush. Doing it boosted my math skills, which proved valuable later in my career. I also worked at the deep sink, washing equipment like the fry machines.

The diversity of the crew was new and exciting. Even though

segregation had long been outlawed, the community was still socially separate. The people I went to school with looked a lot like me, so it was fun getting to know people from different backgrounds and ethnicities at work. We all got along well.

After graduating from the University of South Carolina in 1984 with a degree in journalism, I moved to Winston-Salem and became a media buyer for an advertising agency that happened to have McDonald's as one of its accounts. That was a big deal because McDonald's has a large marketing budget, is particular about who it does business with, and has a reputation for managing its advertising dollars to get the biggest bang for its buck.

One day when I arrived at work I found a letter on my desk from "Uncle Ronald." My boss had apparently spotted a discarded drink cup in my trash that was from a McDonald's competitor. Using the pen name "Uncle Ronald," he let me know that we were expected to demonstrate loyalty to our clients by patronizing their businesses.

The funny part was that I didn't put that cup in my trash. I assume a colleague didn't want to get caught with the evidence. Nevertheless, I was new enough in the job that it scared the heck out of me.

Later in my career, I became the national sales manager for two television stations in North Carolina, selling commercial spots to McDonald's. The company was always looking for opportunities to leverage its marketing dollars. For example, if the company was running a national campaign for one of its products, like salads, the local owner/operators might want to partner in some way with a local health fair and advertise around that. Part of my job was to look for local community events in which McDonald's could also become a partner. This experience helped prepare me for what came next.

The media company reorganized its marketing department in 2005, and I had to choose between relocating from Winston-Salem or finding a new job. The time was right to think about the next chapter in my career. I had grown tired of the advertising rat race and thought about the nonprofit sector. I had been a volunteer and fundraiser for an international women's organization for many years and enjoyed it. I told my husband, "I want to do something that counts."

One day at the post office I ran into a friend whose husband served on the board of one of the other nonprofit organizations I had volunteered with—the local Ronald McDonald House, which provides low-cost or free lodging to the families of children hospitalized with serious illnesses. In fact, I had been active in helping raise money when it was founded in 1984. My friend mentioned that the board was recruiting a development director. My heart skipped a beat. I quickly excused myself, raced home, and anxiously called the House's executive director.

The person who answered said the director was unavailable and, in any event, the window for submitting applications had closed. I immediately faxed my resume anyway. An hour later my phone rang and I spent the next ninety minutes speaking with the executive director. We both knew my McDonald's background was a near-perfect fit, but she wanted to make sure I was truly prepared for the salary cut involved. My husband and I had already discussed it and agreed we could make the sacrifice. I ended up getting the job.

There are so many ways this position has been a great fit and a great gift. I understood from day one a lot of what McDonald's was looking for. I already had relationships with the owner/operators, who are among the most generous supporters of our House. I bring credibility to my presentations to local franchisees. Many of them know me, and I am familiar with the McDonald's lingo and culture. My experience helping connect the company with local events and causes had given me a network of people and organizations I could turn to on behalf of the House.

Our Ronald McDonald House has been in operation now for nearly thirty years. There are a lot of hospitals in the area, serving a widely dispersed population of families. That means there are a lot of families to serve and, thanks to the generosity of others, we recently expanded the Winston-Salem House from seventeen to thirty-five bedrooms.

When I first came to work here, I had no idea how connected I would get to the families. It's one thing to say, "We have thirty-five bedrooms," and list all the amenities. It's another thing to mingle with the guests and even work alongside them.

Just like working on crew at a restaurant, at the House it's a team effort. If you're walking down the hall and you see that somebody needs something, you pitch in. Each family that stays at the House is given a specific chore to do, whether it's taking out the trash or sweeping the front porch. It's important that guests have a sense of responsibility so they feel like part of a family, like they're at home instead of a hotel.

As a result of this system, I get to know the families and I can say to a donor, "Because of your generosity, Sally's mother got a good night's sleep last night in a comfortable bed. She had a wonderful warm breakfast that our volunteers prepared. All this lets her focus her energy on helping Sally at the hospital." There's a real emotional connection.

So I'm still learning valuable lessons, in this case how to *tell* instead of sell.

All the skills I've learned came into play when I had an opportunity to negotiate with an eight-year-old named Serena. She was being treated in Winston-Salem for brain cancer, and her family lived almost a hundred miles away, in the Appalachian foothills.

2012
There are 313 Ronald McDonald Houses, in 32 countries.

My office was located near the handicapped entrance. Every morning I heard Serena's mother, Dinesha, wheeling Serena up the walk on the way back from taking her to the hospital for her early-morning treatment. I got up from my desk to open the door for them. We exchanged greetings and that was about it.

Serena had her mother's sparkling eyes and beautiful smile and wore her hair in cute little pigtails. But when she came back from treatment, she looked so worn out. Her mom was also tired, but she smiled with gratitude at having a comfortable place to stay. I knew she was trying to stay positive for her daughter.

The treatments so exhausted Serena that she slept most of the day. As a result, she was up all night. Dinesha had other children staying at the House with her, so she was up during the day with her other kids, and then up much of the night when Serena was awake and needed attention. It was wearing Dinesha out. The staff and I put our heads together to see if we could find a solution.

Every Wednesday volunteers brought dogs to the House as pet

therapy. Serena missed her dog at home, and I noticed that every Wednesday afternoon, she was wide awake in her wheelchair waiting in the lobby to see those dogs. "If she could stay up one day," I wondered, "maybe we could somehow get her to stay up every day." We asked the therapy dog volunteers if they would each donate a different afternoon so Serena might be able to play with a therapy dog every day. They agreed, and negotiations began in earnest.

"Would you like to see the dogs every day?" I asked her.

Her face lit up. "Yes, ma'am."

"Well, if you want to see the dogs every day, you have to stay up all day."

Serena gave me a thoughtful look and said, "What about half a day?"

"Okay," I said. "Which half of the dog would you like to see?" She gave me one of those looks that said, *I think you just got me.*

Sure enough, she put her mind to staying up. To help her stay awake while she waited for the dogs, we kept her busy stuffing envelopes, going to the local YMCA, going to the Children's Museum, and so on. Serena finally got back on schedule. Mom was happy, and so was Serena.

And then she ditched the wheelchair.

That was three years ago. Serena has been back to visit every year since. Last year she proudly showed me the pink hearing aids she'd gotten to compensate for the hearing loss caused by the cancer.

"Oh, good," I said, admiring them. "Are you minding your mama more because you can hear her better?" She gave me her you-got-me look.

Serena will have to come back for more treatments, so she'll be a guest at the House again. But instead of the exhausted eight-year-old, we've got a smiling eleven-year-old. She's become a budding young lady who has learned to flirt. She is still out of the wheelchair.

My level of compassion has grown in the six years I've been with the Ronald McDonald House. I'm blessed with a healthy child and don't take things for granted as much now. The Ronald McDonald House is a blessing for the families who stay with us and also for those of us who work there.

HIRED 1979

Diana Thomas

AUTHOR'S NOTE

One of the things many people remember about their first experience on a McDonald's crew is that working with a diverse group of people in a service setting and interacting with strangers helped them become more self-confident. Not only did Diana Thomas overcome her teenaged shyness, but she also discovered she had a talent for teaching. She worked for many years in recruiting, human resources, and then training. Today, she is vice president of training, learning, and development for McDonald's USA. Her team runs Hamburger University, the company's eighty-acre training facility in Oak Brook, Illinois. HU, as it is known, is now an accredited academic institution where students can earn up to fifty college credits. It has been the model for similar training facilities in England, Germany, China, Japan, Australia, and Brazil.

I can't remember a time when
I wasn't learning something new.

"What would you like to do here?" the manager asked me during my interview for my first real job, at a company-owned McDonald's restaurant. I was a shy sixteen-year-old with braces. Our family had just moved to Jessup, Maryland, and I was the new kid at school. "You know, something in the back. That would be my preference," I replied.

When I found out I was one of the forty-two kids hired out of 150 who applied, I was so happy, until I went in for my first day. "You're going to be the hostess. The hostess talks to all the customers." I actually felt sick to my stomach. What do you say to customers? They're eating. Why would I interrupt them?

For the first two weeks I kept myself busy cleaning until my supervisor asked me one day, "Are you cleaning the restrooms again? They're fine. Let me show you how to talk to customers."

My career goal was to become a teacher. At the time, McDonald's kids' birthday parties were big. I loved doing those and was good at it, so that's how I found my footing. Then I wanted to learn everything and discovered that McDonald's wanted to teach me everything. I became a crew trainer, then a shift manager, and then a swing manager.

My father was pleased that I was doing so well as a part-timer, but when I got to college and the company wanted me to move up and become a full-time salaried manager, he changed his tune. "I'm not sending you to college to work at McDonald's. I want you to get a real job." He insisted I wait until I graduated and had looked around before deciding. Meanwhile, I was already helping run two different restaurants as a swing manager and going to school full time.

There were many people who were great role models for me. One was restaurant manager Lisa Schultz. I always wanted to be like Lisa. The thing that impressed me about her is that she always kept her commitments. If you asked her for something when she was busy, she wrote it down in her notebook and got back to you later. She never forgot. I thought to myself, "If I get a chance to lead as many people as she does, I want people to think about me in the same way: that I follow through on my commitments."

During my last semester in college I went through a career

assessment and was told I was particularly suited for human resources—called *personnel* back then. I called the McDonald's corporate offices and asked, "Do you have a personnel department?" They did, of course, and I ended up doing an internship in the regional office in Washington, DC. I loved it and worked there for several years after graduation, doing crew and management recruiting as well as working with colleges on career programs.

My career has been different from those who worked for owner/operators. I worked in a market that was about 85 to 90 percent company-owned restaurants. Any time we opened a new location, I was involved. One of the biggest recruiting challenges we've always faced is the bias against McDonald's common among educators. There were a couple of areas where I worked where we had trouble recruiting students from the local high schools. One of the restaurants was right next to a high school, and we still couldn't get any kids on crew. So I went into the high school one day and met the head guidance counselor. She said, "I'm not sending my kids over there. It's a dead-end job."

"I understand," I said. "At one point, my dad thought that." I shared my story with her. It took a while, but I got her to admit that maybe it wasn't so bad. Maybe it was actually a good thing.

When I was ready to be promoted to a human resources manager, my regional manager said, "I want you to think about becoming the training leader in our region instead. I think that would be a good fit for you." I didn't know anything about training, but we made a deal: if I didn't like the training after thirty days, he would let me relocate to another region as the human resources leader.

I had always wanted to be a teacher and discovered I loved training. It became my new career, and I ended up moving to several different regions over several years. Then, nine years ago, I was offered the position of the dean of Hamburger University. As a senior director, my role was to coordinate the other McDonald's Hamburger Universities around the world, so they would have the same standards that the global training center had in place.

Hamburger University in Oak Brook, Illinois, now offers more than fifty college credits for our restaurant management and our mid-management curriculum, almost a year and a half of college credits. It is one of twelve corporate training institutions among the Fortune 100 that has had its courses accredited by the American Council on Education.

My appointment to this position came at a challenging period for the company, in 2002. At one point, the company's stock sank precipitously. *Good to Great* author Jim Collins, in his book *Six Rules for Brand Revitalization*, said it best. We took our eye off our core business. The company made several acquisitions of other quick-service restaurants that proved to be a distraction, and we became isolated from what our customers wanted.

For example, when I had been a manager coaching crew people, if a customer wanted mustard on a Filet-O-Fish sandwich, they were to say, "I'm sorry, that's one of our trade products. We can't do that." I think about it today and realize we had gotten too full of ourselves. We had lost touch with the customers.

I was in the field with one of the division presidents at the time the company was struggling and realized they were looking for a silver bullet to fix our problems. They didn't seem to understand that we had moved away from holding our restaurants accountable for adhering to the quality, service, and cleanliness standards. Once we got rid of the other distractions, we started to listen to the customers again.

I had the chance at the time to work directly with Jim Cantalupo, the company's CEO who had retired but was recruited to come back and lead a turnaround. He wanted to meet with anybody who had recently come from the restaurant front lines. He was a great listener and asked some great questions: "What do you hear are the challenges in the field? What frustrated you? What could we be doing differently?" To be part of the home office when that transition was happening was rewarding and exciting.

When the company divided into two—domestic and international—I became the vice president of training, learning, and development and was responsible for overseeing training for McDonald's USA. That is where I've been for the last nine years. Being in a classroom, training the trainers, the senior directors, and the directors who oversee training, I get to do what I always wanted to and have the opportunity to travel.

Growing up, I never left the state of Maryland. Now I've been all over the world to see all the Hamburger Universities. I think about the things that I have been exposed to and how much broader the world is for my daughters.

My dad, who had wanted me to get a real job after college, is one of my biggest fans. He even went to work at a McDonald's as a maintenance person when he retired and got bored. It's been an evolution for both of us.

DID YOU KNOW?

In 1961, Fred Turner, McDonald's former senior chairman and Ray Kroc's first grill man, founded Hamburger University in the basement of a McDonald's restaurant in Elk Grove Village, Illinois. The first class of fifteen students graduated in 1961. Today, more than 5,000 students attend Hamburger University each year.

There are currently six Hamburger University locations around the world, in Oak Brook, London, Shanghai, Munich, Tokyo, Sydney, and São Paulo.

1980s

HIRED 1980

Cody Teets

EDITOR'S NOTE

Five years ago, in August 2007, I first spoke with Cody Teets about her idea for this book and immediately recognized its potential. Here was an opportunity to turn a popular misconception upside down (the dead-end McJob) and to remind ourselves as a nation that at the beginning of every success story there is an entry-level job. Best of all, Cody was the perfect person to write it. Her compelling personal story, growing up in modest circumstances with a strong work ethic, gives her unique credibility. —*Foster Winans*

The sky's the limit. Shoot for the moon.
Even if you fall short, you will land among the stars.

My restaurant career officially began at a competitor across the street from the McDonald's where I first joined the company thirty-two years ago. At the time, Der Wienerschnitzel, a hamburger and hot dog place in Denver, was the only employer I knew of that would hire fourteen-year-olds. A friend who was a few months older than me worked there, and that's how I got hired. Before then I did babysitting to earn my own money, which my mother let me keep. It was a big deal to have my own money.

My parents divorced when I was four, and my mother, two younger sisters, and I lived with my grandparents. From elementary school until junior high, the paychecks from my mother's jobs couldn't cover our expenses. To make ends meet, we received welfare assistance and food stamps and often bought our clothes at Goodwill.

As the oldest, I was responsible for helping my mother with my little sisters. When we went grocery shopping, it was my job to keep track of how much we spent. I used a red plastic calculator to make sure we didn't go over and have to put something back.

My mom is my hero. She set the bar high early on, pushing me to earn good grades, work hard, and follow through on anything I started. When I fell short of a goal and took it out on myself, she'd say, "Don't quit. You can do whatever you want to do. The sky's the limit." If I wanted to call in sick to spend time with my friends, she'd remind me I had a responsibility to my employer and coworkers. She and my grandmother Cody, a bank executive, were role models for navigating the business world at a time when girls and women were discouraged from showing strength.

Some of the experiences I had working at Der Wienerschnitzel were similar to those that crew members have at McDonald's and just as formative. My girlfriend had turned fifteen and had the key to the restaurant because we were the opening crew. If we didn't show up, the restaurant didn't open. That was a lot of responsibility for a couple of kids. One morning she was too sick to work and called me to come get the key and open on my own. I was nervous, but I knew how to do everything.

I worked every chance I got, and my mother and grandparents praised me for my initiative at such a young age. But my mother worried. "Don't you want to just take time to be a kid and enjoy yourself? Don't you want to go out for cheerleading?"

I was happy working and didn't feel I was missing out on anything. If I went out for cheerleading, I'd just have to spend my hard-earned money on a uniform.

As soon as I turned sixteen, I got a job at the McDonald's across the street where my girlfriend had worked since she turned sixteen. That was October 1, 1980. It was a lot busier than Der Wienerschnitzel, and there were more incentives for doing a good job. The employees and the managers were friendlier and more of my friends from school ate there.

The owner/operator, Bob Charles, was known as a marketing innovator in the McDonald's system. He was an early adopter of the drive-thru and went on to add second and third druve-thru windows to make service more efficient. To motivate his crews, he designed a bingo-like card and once you had learned a station, you got a checkmark. When you'd filled in a row, you'd get a pin or a free meal or a bonus.

I'd only been there three months when I was employee of the month out of about fifty people who worked there. It was fun, I loved it, and

I decided to learn everything I could so I could become a swing manager and work my way through college, aiming for a degree in marketing. I became a zealous recruiter for our McDonald's restaurants. In my high school yearbook it says I was "most likely to marry Ronald McDonald."

When I was eighteen I became a swing-shift manager. Being in charge came naturally to me. I had a lot of practice as the oldest child. The experience had prepared me on how to talk to coworkers in a way that would get them to do what was needed. From time to time, a manager might ask me to be in charge of the grill or service areas or to determine the food production needed during a rush. Those were important roles because you had to coordinate two groups of people to make sure there was enough food being produced to meet the demand. Those were great lessons for becoming a leader people would listen to and respect.

I worked at the restaurant all through college and when I graduated from the University of Colorado with my marketing degree (with a minor in accounting), I started interviewing for jobs with advertising agencies. I quickly discovered that I'd have to take a big salary cut, so I decided to stay at McDonald's and see what developed.

One of the many people who mentored me along the way was a field consultant named Roger Kennan, who was a model of leadership for me. By the time I met him, I had gone from crew person to area supervisor, in charge of five restaurants and training for the twelve-restaurant organization. I was looking for input on how to motivate teams. I set high standards for myself and demanded it from those who worked for me. However, my efforts at motivating the team were draining. I suspected that at times my attempts were having the opposite effect.

Roger was wise about human nature and he knew the specific culture of the company. I explained my concerns, and he pointed out that a leader can't manage everyone the same way. Every person is motivated differently, and a leader or supervisor's job is to figure out what it is that makes each person tick and try to get at the root of that. "If certain people are motivated by time off, then give them more time off. If some people are motivated by money, give them more money. Don't try to create an incentive program that rewards them all the same."

This advice hit home when my operator, Bob Charles, offered to assist me in becoming an owner/operator myself. At the time, I could not fathom ever having enough money to buy a restaurant and it proved to be a turning point—I decided to work for McDonald's Corporation instead.

One of the most important lessons I've learned, and continue to work on, is to fight the urge to see everything as either black or white. In any large organization, rules and procedures are important, but there may be room for negotiation. I've found that at certain times, it's more effective to manage in the gray areas.

Another lesson was how to deal with people in a way that preserves their dignity, even when they've fallen short of expectations. The long-term goal is for both people to walk out head held high. This is something that I continue to think about when working with people today.

Also, I've learned you can't do everything by yourself. In this environment you have to rely on others to help you accomplish your goals. All the lessons I learned early in life have enabled me to pay it forward with the many people I work with today.

Quick-service restaurants provide the first real jobs for millions of teenagers each year. It's both a challenge and an opportunity. It's honest work, it can be fun, and if you pay attention, you'll learn skills that will help you throughout your life.

DID YOU KNOW?

1980: Chicken McNuggets went into test marketing.

HIRED 1980

Jeffrey P. Bezos

AUTHOR'S NOTE

Lists of famous people who worked at McDonald's always include Amazon.com founder Jeff Bezos. Few people know that his father had worked there as well, when *he* was a teenager. While Jeff was understandably too busy for a live interview, he did provide some answers to a few key questions. One of his oft-repeated quotes about learning how to crack eggs seems consistent with the single most important component of his business—the logistics of moving things quickly from seller to customer without damaging them.

Jeff's father, Miguel "Mike" Bezos, emigrated from Cuba alone in 1962 when he was fifteen. He was one of thousands of children sent to the US by their parents around the time of the Cuban missile crisis. He and about a dozen other Cuban teens lived in a Catholic mission in Delaware, learning English and earning their high school diplomas. A family spokesman confirmed that Mike did indeed work at McDonald's in the sixties at a location near the University of Maryland, College Park.

You learn a lot as a teenager working at McDonald's. It's different from what you learn in school. Don't underestimate the value of that!

I ended up working at a McDonald's in Miami because I needed a summer job. My dad had always told stories about his McDonald's experience as a teenager. I filled out an application when I was sixteen. My dad loved it—he was reminded of his own experience at the Golden Arches.

My first week on the job, a five-gallon, wall-mounted ketchup dispenser got stuck open in the kitchen and dumped a prodigious quantity of ketchup into every hard-to-reach kitchen crevice. Since I was the new guy, they handed me the cleaning solution and said, "Get going!"

I was a grill man and never worked the cash registers. The most challenging thing was keeping everything going at the right pace during a rush. One of the great gifts I got from that job is that I learned to crack eggs with one hand. My favorite shift was Saturday morning. The first thing I would do is get a big bowl and crack three hundred eggs into it.

One of the things that was really fun about working at McDonald's was to get really fast at all of this stuff. See how many eggs you can crack in a period of time and still not get any shell in them.

The manager at my McDonald's was excellent. He had a lot of teenagers working for him, and he kept us focused even while we had fun.

You can learn responsibility in any job, if you take it seriously. You learn a lot as a teenager working at McDonald's. It's different from what you learn in school. Don't underestimate the value of that!

SETH POPPEL/YEARBOOK LIBRARY

HIRED 1981

Bridgett Freeman

AUTHOR'S NOTE

You'd think that working for McDonald's for twenty-five years and rising to become senior executives would make owning a restaurant a piece of cake, but Bridgett Freeman and her husband, Bruce, found the transition from paycheck to payroll a challenge. They both had successful careers on the corporate side when they decided to become owner/operators in 2007. Their journey is unusual because they met and married as employees and because they chose to give up the benefits of a stable corporate income to become entrepreneurs.

People have to learn to be successful. You have to help them understand how they can take an average job and turn it into an opportunity.

My introduction to McDonald's was through my older sister who worked in a restaurant in Baltimore. After her first day she came home full of stories about how the managers and crew made it so much fun. Every day after that, I couldn't wait until she would come home from work and tell us all about it.

The first time I went there when my sister was working was so exciting and unforgettable—all the timers going off, the fast pace, the manager giving out directions, and me thinking, "What's behind that counter? I have to get behind that counter to see what they're doing back there." It reminded me of the circus with the ringmaster shouting instructions to all the performers.

On Fridays the manager took the crew bowling. I always wanted to go with my sister, but I wasn't old enough. Finally, one time my mother said I could go. While I waited in the restaurant for them to get ready, I could hear them laughing in the back. It was killing me, so I said to the manager, "Would you let me come behind the counter if I sweep and mop and wipe things down? Can I please go back there?" When he said that I could, it was like angels singing.

The age that you're allowed to work at McDonald's is sixteen. Every day that my mom would take my sister to work, I would go and ask the manager when I could start. The answer was always, "You're not old enough yet." But one day the answer was finally yes, and I ran out to the car where my mother was waiting and shouted, "Oh, my God! Oh, my God! They're going to let me work for McDonald's!"

Getting that job was about becoming responsible and about competing with my sister, who was a perfectionist at everything. My first day on the French fry station, I kind of goofed it up. My sister said, "You're moving too slow." I thought to myself, "I'm going to show you." I learned how to make those French fries and became the best French fry person they had.

When I was in high school, I played softball until I had to choose between my sports commitment and McDonald's. All of my friends stuck with the sports, but after some soul searching I decided to stick with McDonald's. After school, I would get my book and head to work. Some of my friends would tease me from time to time. "Oh, are you still working for McDonald's?" I didn't care. I loved my job.

Over the years as I progressed to a swing manager, a second assistant, and so on, I would run into those same friends, and they would say,

"What are you doing still working for McDonald's?" They would tease me about the uniforms.

When I got promoted to first assistant position, they kept at it. "Tell me you're not still working for McDonald's!"

"Oh, yes, I am still working for McDonald's."

When I was promoted to the next level, manager of a $3.3 million restaurant in Maryland, they said, "You're still working for McDonald's? Is that the best you can do?"

"Hey," I said. "I'm twenty-three and I'm managing a $3.3 million business. What are you doing?"

When I got to the supervisory level with a company car and an expense account, I'd say, "Well, I'm now supervising seven restaurants. What are you doing?" It took four or five promotions before they finally figured out that I was doing just fine.

1980

Ted Turner launches CNN, the first all-news network.

Later, when I became a training consultant for the company, I had the revelation that people do not choose to be unsuccessful. They have to learn how to be successful. You have to help them understand how they can take an average job and turn it into an opportunity. That's been my experience—McDonald's helped me identify my best qualities and to develop and use skills I didn't know I had.

My husband and I met when he was transferred to Baltimore as an operations manager. We started dating and eventually got married. We each have nearly thirty years in the business.

We relocated to Atlanta in 2002 where Bruce was director of operations and I was a regional training consultant. I was promoted to regional training manager in 2004. My department was responsible for facilitating classes for the 731 McDonald's restaurants located in Georgia, Alabama, South Carolina, and Chattanooga, Tennessee.

In 2007 we took the leap from employees to employers. We bought a franchise in Macon, Georgia. Our first restaurant was brand new and we decided to hire only crew members and managers that had no experience so we could train them from the ground up. That made it a challenging experience. A little more than thirty days after we opened our first restaurant, we took over a restaurant within a Walmart. Then we opened another brand-new restaurant in another location, all this taking place in about three and a half months. Today, we have four locations and will break ground in 2012 on number five.

We were able to grow so rapidly because we had received the great one-on-one training from crew on up. We divide our responsibilities according to our individual strengths. My focus is crew and management, people development, and daily operations. Bruce manages the back office—financial matters, marketing, and community relations.

Bruce says that there are days when it seems like it was easier being in charge of 425 restaurants than owning four. We discovered that, compared with being an owner/operator, working for the corporation was a breeze. We'd always had an umbrella over us that we forgot was there.

We have learned a lot about ourselves, including that we like the independence and autonomy that comes with being owners. There is a sense of pride you get driving onto your own parking lot that you can never experience as an employee.

In the nearly five years we've been franchisees, we've received numerous awards and recognition from McDonald's Corporation, and our employees have been recognized as well. We've had two winners of the Ray Kroc Award, the highest award that a manager can receive.

Two of my pleasures are seeing people I helped train move ahead and do well, and getting calls from people I've helped asking me for advice all these years later.

There is a third, which is getting to go behind the counter now anytime I want.

DID YOU KNOW

1981: The McRib sandwich went into test marketing.

HIRED 1982

Marlene González

AUTHOR'S NOTE

Thirty years ago this year, a fifteen-year-old Venezuelan girl stopped in at a McDonald's in Virginia to see if she could get some part-time work where she could save for college. The remarkable career that followed took her around the world and up the ladder to one of the most complex jobs in the company—in charge of global training and executive development for 2.5 million employees working in 30,000 restaurants located in more than one hundred countries. She says one of the most valuable lessons she learned along the way was how to coach and mentor others to be their best. Today, she is doing just that as an entrepreneur, running her own consulting firm working with Fortune 500 companies to help them develop their talent into top producers and leaders.

I learned from being a restaurant manager that
I needed to be persistent and consistent.
There are no shortcuts and no mysteries to it.

One of my most embarrassing moments working as a crew person came on my second day when I fried a couple of weeks' worth of cherry pies all at once. There was this whole lingo I had to learn when people were giving orders and asking for things. I hadn't learned it yet and was being trained in the kitchen. I was by myself when one of the managers called out, "Could you put down a cherry pie?"

For some reason I could not understand what he was saying. Instead of frying one cherry pie, I decided to do a whole basket, which could hold about twenty pies. We only sold one or two cherry pies a day.

When the manager came back to the kitchen and saw what I'd done, he was livid. His wastage report was going to be over the top for that day. I was close to tears when he calmed down and told me, "I understand. It's your second day. It's not your fault. I'm really so sorry." We both were, and things got steadily better from then on.

My first McDonald's job was in Alexandria, Virginia, while I was in high school. I was fifteen years old, and it was the only place I could find that was hiring part-timers. I wanted to save some money for college, and the flexibility made it possible to work and go to school. I also liked the restaurant, the people working there, and the environment—it was fast paced and fun.

My family was living in the Washington, DC, area because my father was a diplomat working in the Venezuelan embassy. I grew up in Venezuela and, given my father's profession, our family knew we would eventually move back home.

When I got the McDonald's job, my father was initially upset. "Why are you going to clean restaurants? I'm not sending you to college to clean restaurants or attend to customers at a register." Once he understood that McDonald's was a large, reputable company and the leader in its field, he got on board and became my biggest advocate.

My first restaurant manager was Carlos Cornejo. He was an inspirational mentor from whom I learned a lot of very important lessons. He was sociable and charismatic and took the time to get to know every single employee. I remember him walking into the restaurant and approaching each crew person, saying, "Hi!" and asking, "How are you today?" or "How was school?" It was small talk, but it left a powerful impression that he was on your side.

After I had been there awhile, Carlos recommended me for the crew leader position. As crew leader, I was responsible for two or three individuals in a specific area of the restaurant, like the drive-thru, front area, or kitchen. I trained the team and was their resource and backup. This was a training ground for me to develop and demonstrate leadership, initiative, and teamwork, as well as show that I had communication skills, understood the operations, and focused on the customer. At fifteen years old, it was challenging and exciting to be in charge of other people. Being given so much responsibility made me feel on top of the world.

I had plans to go on to college after high school, but when I graduated my father's assignment was over and we returned to Venezuela. I had worked at McDonald's for three years and gotten a lot of great training and experience.

Then, fate stepped in. I was going through college applications back home and saw that a McDonald's was opening in Venezuela. So I decided to visit the restaurant just out of curiosity, to see if it was similar to the one where I'd worked. Not only did it look familiar, but there was Carlos Cornejo, my manager from Alexandria!

"Oh, my God!" he said. "This is destiny. You have to come back to McDonald's. We're looking for managers."

It was totally unexpected. We strolled around the parking lot while he and the owner interviewed me, and I was hired on the spot to be a fast-track manager for McDonald's Venezuela. So I was doing what I'd planned, working and going to college, only it was in Venezuela. I was in my twenties and managing a $2.5 million business. That helped prepare me for my future positions with the company and beyond.

I met my husband, Carlos González, at McDonald's in Venezuela. We were on similar career paths. He had worked at McDonald's when he was in high school in Winnetka, Illinois, and then came back to Venezuela. We got married in 1989. Soon after, we were offered the opportunity to work for McDonald's Corporation in the international division.

Carlos and I weren't sure at first but when I asked my parents for advice, my father immediately said, "Go! McDonald's is a great company.

You'll just have to be flexible and be willing to travel the world and relocate to take advantage of the opportunity."

Two weeks later, we found ourselves in Chile, helping an owner/operator recruit staff and find suppliers. We were there for a year setting up the operations, training managers, and working with the owner/operator.

Then we got a call asking us to go to Mexico. My husband was in operations, and I was in training. I was twenty-seven and in charge of training, expanding the McOpCo operation for the country. We lived and worked in Mexico for five years.

In the 1990s, McDonald's began expanding its international efforts and that created many new openings. I happened to be in the right place at the right time, doing the right things. We loved Mexico and were about to buy a house when I got a call from the home office asking me if I would relocate to Illinois and take a job at Hamburger University. I decided to take the risk and, for the first time, worked in a corporate environment in the US.

Although I understood that McDonald's was big and growing, it became real when I first joined Hamburger University. To do business globally, one of our biggest challenges was how to train people from ninety countries, speaking forty different languages, and working in more than 20,000 restaurants.

My training as a restaurant manager proved valuable. I understood how to coach and mentor others to be their best so they could reach their goals and produce good results. I also had learned from being a manager that I needed to be persistent and consistent. There are no shortcuts and no mysteries to it.

I worked at McDonald's for twenty-five years, posted at various times in the US, the UK, Germany, France, and throughout Latin America. This gave me a truly global perspective. I held a variety of executive positions during these years, including management, operations, product development and innovation, and franchising and field service.

My final three years I was senior director of global training, learning, and development and worked with Hamburger Universities around the world. My husband is still an officer of the company, vice president of McDonald's Latin America Operations.

I'm now an entrepreneur myself. In 2007, I started a consulting practice working with government, nonprofit, and Fortune 500 companies, coaching and training their executives and agents. I also co-authored a book for Latino professionals. I am living my dream.

DID YOU KNOW?

1982: Soft serve cones added to the menu.
The Commodore 64 home computer is introduced.

HIRED 1982

Susan Singleton

Parents bring their kids into our restaurants and there is some surprise when we don't automatically hire everybody that walks in.

The economy was in rough shape in 1982 when I graduated from the University of Illinois with a degree in restaurant management and business. My first post-grad job was as a hostess at a casual dining restaurant across the street from where Hamburger University was at that time, in Elk Grove Village. The people taking classes would frequently come in to eat. One day a group of men showed up wearing suits and ties, a bit dressier than the usual crowd.

"What do you do for McDonald's?" I asked. They told me they were owner/operators. That rang a bell for me. My father was an executive with Seagram's Distillery, so he had a natural interest in the restaurant business. When I was a teenager, he had talked about how great it would be to own a McDonald's like the one in our neighborhood. It was always busy.

When I got home that night I told my father that I might be interested in seeing what the possibilities were.

"Well, if you want us to try to figure out how to own a McDonald's, you might as well start by going to work there."

I answered an ad for an assistant manager for an organization that owned restaurants in Des Plaines, Illinois, where Ray Kroc launched the company. I interviewed and got the job, and that's how I got started in McDonald's.

When I was in high school, working at McDonald's was very popular. By 1982, though, a lot of my friends had gone on to start their careers, and they thought it was kind of pathetic that I wound up working at McDonald's. They thought I could have done better. But I enjoyed the fast pace. I had worked at Busch Gardens in Tampa, Florida, while I was in college. Like McDonald's, Busch Gardens was a busy place with lots of different things happening at once. That environment appealed to me.

The fellow who had interviewed me was the area supervisor for the group of restaurants. He'd started with McDonald's in 1976. When I reported for duty my first day, he said, "I think that I'm going to do your training myself." Exactly a week later, he asked me to marry him. That was twenty-nine years ago, and it worked out fine.

My husband, Chris, loved everything about McDonald's and wanted us to become owner/operators. In 1985, three years after I started work at

McDonald's, we applied and were offered a location that was in need of a makeover in the city of Chicago. The previous owner had passed away, and the company was looking for a couple to give the restaurant a little TLC. My owner/operator at the time had recommended Chris and me, telling the company, "I've got a perfect couple for you. A young couple without a lot of money but lots of operational experience."

The restaurant was a bit of an orphan. It was the lowest volume freestanding McDonald's in the Chicago area, located in a predominantly Orthodox Jewish neighborhood, next door to a Jewish mikveh. Our customers were from many different cultures—Filipino, Indian, Israeli, Palestinian, and Russian.

We knew we had our work cut out for us the first night we owned it. A group of Orthodox women came in and said, "We need a Gentile girl to be our Shabbos goy." In Jewish tradition, only a non-Jew can turn the lights on and off during the Sabbath, which starts on Friday night.

I raised my hand, thinking this was good customer relations, and said I'd help out. They said, "We're sorry we can't eat here. You're not kosher, but we bless you." So I learned a little something about Jewish culture and did my duty, going over there every Friday night to hear them apologize for not being customers and bless me.

From October to May we remodeled the restaurant from the ground up. Then we had a grand reopening. My husband and I already had a baby girl, and I was pregnant with our son. We'd just signed the mortgage for a little house, and we were on the path to making our dream happen.

That's when the city decided to close the road in front of our restaurant—a whole city block. Then they dug an eight-foot trench down the middle for a new sewer. People couldn't reach us and business tanked. We were going out of our minds.

My dad said his accountant was friends with someone at McDonald's and we should call him up to see if he could help us. Whether it was naïveté or desperation, we called the "someone at McDonald's" and asked if we could make an appointment to see him and explain what had happened to us. He said he'd be glad to meet with us.

We drove to the company's headquarters in Oak Brook and were told to go to the eighth floor. Chris and I started to put it together when the elevator doors opened onto the executive suite. The man we were going to see was Gerald Newman, the chief accounting officer for the entire company, worldwide.

We began to explain our dilemma.

"I know about you kids already," he said. "My sister lives nearby, and she told me how much you cleaned everything up. I'm going to reduce your rent, and I'm going to help you build a gravel road in the alley so people can get into your parking lot from the next street."

My husband and I started crying. We couldn't believe it.

He said, "My goal is for you two to eventually be so successful, you'll pay me back tenfold. I'm not worried about it."

And sure enough that's what happened. He helped get the gravel road built, and we've been paying it forward ever since.

We immediately started marketing the heck out of the restaurant and wound up doing more business during the three months the street was closed than the restaurant had done in the entire previous year with the road open. Even Ed Rensi, who was the president of McDonald's USA at the time, came out to see what was happening.

What started as a horrible situation ended up being a great opportunity, letting me meet the top management at McDonald's, people with whom I have developed lifelong relationships. A week before his sudden death from a heart attack at age sixty-one, five years after we bought the location, Gerry Newman had stopped by to check in on us, as he did from time to time.

He would look at my profit-and-loss statements every month to make sure we were doing okay. When we finally crossed $100,000 in sales for one month, a big achievement for us, he wrote us a personal note. There were 10,000 restaurants at the time, and he took the time to write to us. To this day, because of that, there isn't anything that I wouldn't do to give back to a fellow McDonald's person.

The restaurant business is never a walk in the park, and there were times when Chris and I wondered whether we'd have been happier working for someone else. But the pleasures have been great, like watching some of our employees become successful. For example, I had a manager, Eduardo Vasquez, who started to work for us twelve years ago knowing not a word of English. Today, he runs one of my restaurants and will be a supervisor someday. I look at what he can provide for his family now, and he's just one of many.

Recruiting young people was tough in the 1990s to the early 2000s. But in the last four or five years, things have changed significantly. Parents bring their sixteen- and seventeen-year-old kids into our restaurants, saying, "You need to try to get a job here." There is some surprise on the parents' end when we don't automatically hire everybody who walks in. I think they have the expectation that we're going to take their kid no matter what. After all, they think, "It's just McDonald's." But that's a misperception. Now we're able to be much more selective with our hiring than during any of the twenty-five years that I've been an operator.

When the economy turned sour, we had people coming to work at McDonald's who had been on other career paths and seemed to think it would be a breeze. Many are surprised to find how hard the work is.

DID YOU KNOW?

1982: Ray Kroc celebrates his 80th birthday. Michael Jackson releases the album *Thriller*.

HIRED 1983

Laurieann Gibson

AUTHOR'S NOTE

Ray Kroc encouraged employees to think of themselves as performers, the restaurant as their stage, and the customers as their audience. Laurieann Gibson fit right in when she started her McDonald's job. She was a young dance student who saw in the running of a restaurant a kind of choreographed ballet. Many of the lessons she says she learned as a crew member helped her achieve her phenomenal success. She is an internationally acclaimed choreographer for the biggest stars in the music world, and a star herself—an award-winning performer, composer of movement, and director. Like actress Andie MacDowell, Laurieann saved her earnings to buy a bus ticket to New York, where her remarkable career took off.

For a long time, no one ever knew about my humble beginnings. Now it's something I like to tell people.

I had an emotional attachment to McDonald's well before I started working there. From the age of seven, on Saturdays after dance class, my mother would treat me to a Happy Meal and a sugar donut. I even got to meet Ronald McDonald, an experience every child treasures. Years later I got to meet him again, under very different circumstances. That brought back a lot of positive memories, and inspired me to start sharing them with others. I always get a wide-eyed "No way!" when I tell people I got my start flipping burgers.

My mother and father are first-generation Jamaican–Canadians who immigrated to Toronto as a young couple and raised three girls, me being the youngest. My father was an electrician who worked for an alarm company. He had a company car that we girls hated because it was an ugly yellow with a big purple Federal Alarms sticker on it. It was embarrassing to get dropped off at school in that, and even more so when we would go somewhere dressed up. I had to learn early to ignore what others thought of me.

When I was old enough to start wanting to buy my own clothes, my mother made it clear I would have to earn some of the money. Through a friend, I heard about jobs at McDonald's and interviewed at a new restaurant in the Eaton Centre, a large mall in Toronto that was the place to work. When I was hired, it gave me a feeling of independence that made my friends a little envious.

Going through the training program felt like joining a family that was teaching me about business. They taught tactics like suggestive selling that left a big impression on me and have been useful in my career. I liked the way they were organized, that there was a schedule and responsibility, and that the crew members took pride in what they were doing.

If I was late or missed a shift, it was a big deal. That also taught me about truth and honor—I found out the hard way that you couldn't lie. There was an occasion when I tried. "My mom's in the hospital. That's why I can't get to work." I felt so bad when they found me out and reprimanded me. I didn't want to get fired, so I learned to be punctual. Situations like that when you're young teach character qualities you carry with you for the rest of your life.

Working at McDonald's was a great lesson for someone going into the entertainment business because in both endeavors everybody depends on everybody else to do their job for the end result to be a success. You might say my choreography training began at McDonald's. In a way, a restaurant is a choreographed activity, from the moment somebody comes in to the moment they leave with their food all packaged up. And I had it down! I would dance over to the fries and put them in the bag just the right way, making sure not to touch them. That's part of what made it fun for me—I danced my way through my shifts. And once I got comfortable, I choreographed others.

For example, when the restaurant was busy and there were two of us girls on the registers side by side, we would kind of dance as we worked. "Okay," we'd say in unison as our customers ordered. Then we synchronized pushing the buttons. We'd dance our way through the whole line of customers.

Dance was my life, so I had no notions about going on to university. There was no blueprint for my dream. Nobody we knew could tell us how you could make it as a dancer, or that there was even such a thing as a choreographer or a creative director. But my parents were behind me anyway. If that was what I wanted, they would encourage me. They wanted to make sure that we kids had the opportunity to explore our passions because they missed out on that being young parents.

Along the way there were always negative voices, some inside my head, and some not. "You're working at McDonald's?" people would say. "How is that going to help you make it?"

My answer was always, "Don't you worry about that, because I'm cashing my McDonald's check every two weeks." I invested that money in myself. When my mother couldn't pay for those extra dance classes downtown and when I started taking acting and makeup classes and getting my head shots done, McDonald's paid for all of it.

Some of the young people I worked with gave up and left because it was too much responsibility or they didn't like the way the other kids were laughing at them or they didn't feel it was glamorous enough. Those same people are amazed that someone could go from crew to where I am now. I tell them I was working on getting here all the time. I was learning to see something all the way through. That's how I earned the life

I have—and I'm just getting started!

When I was seventeen, I was accepted into the foreign student program at the prestigious Alvin Ailey American Dance Theater in New York. My McDonald's friends and coworkers were excited at first, and then a little skeptical.

"Hey! You're gettin' out! That's great. Wait, what do you mean you're going to New York?"

"I'm really going. I told you guys I would do this."

"But . . . you mean . . . you're really going?"

My mother was nervous. "Mom, don't worry," I told her. "I'll be fine. No matter what, you can be sure that at nine o'clock in the morning, you'll know exactly where I am—in my ballet classes."

My sister helped me pack two suitcases and a duffel bag, and I got on that bus all by myself. New York proved to be just as big a challenge as it's reputed to be, but I found work in a diner and was on my way to the career of my dreams.

The discipline I learned at McDonald's helped me to survive in a place and in a profession where no one tells you to be on time. They're actually waiting for you not to be responsible, so an opportunity will open and someone else can get it. New York is not a place where someone is going to teach you. It's a place where lots of people are hoping for you to fail. New York will eat you alive if you don't have discipline.

Today, I'm working in what people consider the most glamorous industry, but it's still a business. If a dancer or a musician doesn't show up for Lady Gaga, the performance is affected. Now I'm the manager teaching young people the same thing that they were teaching me at McDonald's. "You can't be late for this rehearsal, or we're all affected."

Years later, after I had become successful, I was asked to participate in an *Essence* magazine music festival in New Orleans. The artists included Mary J. Blige and Gladys Knight, and the sponsor was McDonald's! Among other things, I was to dance in front of some 20,000 people with Ronald McDonald.

I had choreographed all of Mary J. Blige's first videos, so she came right over to me when she spotted me backstage. "What are you doing here? I didn't hire you!"

"I'm hanging out with Ronald McDonald."

"Oh, my God!" she said. "McDonald's is paying you? You've really made it!"

What's funny about that is none of them knew at that time that I had ever worked at McDonald's as a kid. In fact, no one ever knew about my humble beginnings, the stuff I had to do to survive. It was just one of those things that I tucked in my heart. But they did find out later, and now it's something I like to tell people. I love going into a McDonald's and telling the people at the register that I used to do what they do. They're always wide-eyed with disbelief.

The fellow who was Ronald McDonald was impressive. He was serious about his makeup and rehearsal, and he had been Ronald McDonald for some fifteen years. The pride he took in being Ronald and putting magic in kids' hearts was impressive. It was a thrill to work with him.

Even though I was never a manager at McDonald's, I learned a lot from observing, and it has helped shape my managerial style. A lot of dancers who turn choreographers and then become, like myself, a creative director don't understand how to manage artists, the creative team, the record companies, and all the emotions around all of it.

I've worked with many artists—Alicia Keys, Missy Elliott, the Dixie Chicks, the Jonas Brothers. When I started with Lady Gaga, she was an unsigned artist who had been dropped from two major labels. I sensed I could manage this girl's dream and creatively produce it. That confidence came from observing how managers at the restaurant kept it together during a big shift with a lot of people.

People often ask me how I got to where I am. "How did you make it?" "How do you have your own company?" "How did you start as a dancer?" "How did you get a deal to develop artists?"

I say, "You know what? I started at McDonald's. I learned to deal with people from all walks of life, all situations, all nationalities, all personalities—rude people, nasty people, nice people—and they never broke me."

I would tell any young person today, regardless of their circumstances or ambitions, to go get a job at McDonald's because it will provide you with a valuable education. In order to lead, you've got to first understand what it's like to serve. A lot of people think you can just pass it by, but the greatest leaders know how to serve.

People often guess my path was easy. They think maybe I grew up in the business, or had a connection or the financial backing to get the best training, or that I got lucky when I met Puff Daddy or worked with MTV or with Lady Gaga. The answer is none of the above. I worked hard and saw it all the way through.

DID YOU KNOW?

1983: Chicken McNuggets added to the menu.

LTC Michael D. Grice, USMC

AUTHOR'S NOTE

McDonald's is often compared to a military organization because it is managed in a structured way with clear chains of command and consistent procedures. On his way to a successful career as a Marine officer, Mike Grice says much of what he learned about working in a high-pressure environment, being a good crew member, and being an inspiring manager was directly applicable in his professional life. Those lessons served him well during his tours of duty in Afghanistan, where he had to coordinate his unit with multiple coalition partners.

I learned that success meant being the person who requires the least managing. It's what I teach my officers, my Marines, and the people I work with.

L ong before I had a real job, I worked. I had worked for my grandparents on their Colorado farm when I was ten years old, helping them cut wheat and driving a big combine machine. I drove a wheat truck when I was twelve. I was always doing something, whether it was delivering papers or odd jobs.

To me, working was a form of emancipation. Getting an allowance was one thing, but being responsible and earning money on my own was an opportunity for me to stand on my own two feet.

My siblings and I were latchkey kids. My mother was a teacher and a single parent and at times worked three jobs to make ends meet. She was a child of the Depression. Having grown up dirt poor in southeastern Colorado, the principal lesson I learned from her is that you need to make your own way, and if you wanted things you needed to go find a way to get them.

Like any other red-blooded American male, I wanted to get a car and all the other things you want when you're fifteen and sixteen. The only way I was going to get them was with a job. That ended up being McDonald's, where I worked off and on for nine years, starting in 1983.

I had been in other places looking for work and compared to all of them, McDonald's had their act together. You came in, you got an application, you filled out an application, and you talked to a manager. The manager made an appointment for you to come back for an interview. It was the real world.

I got my 100-percent-polyester green uniform and my yellow name tag with Velcro on the back and my paper hat, and then they said, "Well, you're a guy, so you get to work on the grill."

First, though, they sent me down into the basement for my orientation. They had an ancient VCR with cassettes the size of a hardback book. I put a tape in and watched the "Welcome to McDonald's" video to learn the rules of the road. Their concept of training was not to just throw you in, but to sit you down and teach the basics. I was getting paid for it, so I thought it was kind of neat.

I was in awe of the guys who had been there longer than I had and who were so incredibly proficient at what they did. My world narrowed down to one goal: I wanted to be the best burger-flipper I could be.

My first lunch rush was mystifying. I was at the dress table—where they started everybody out—putting mustard, ketchup, onions, and pickles on the Quarter Pounders. As I was putting sandwiches together, I looked around, and it was me and half a dozen other guys all working like it was a synchronized dance.

McDonald's was a meritocracy. You were recognized by the skills you had acquired, not by whose kid you were or who your friends were. Their best employees got the best raises. There was a sense of pride and accomplishment to be able to say, "Yeah, I can do that."

You worked your way up the ladder to the most critical position on crew—"running the bin," or production. In those days, the bin was the heated place where they kept all the sandwiches after they were made. They don't do it that way anymore, but back then the production person would stand in front of the bin and tell people what to make in anticipation of what was going to sell because the food could only sit in the bin for ten minutes.

I learned that to be an effective leader, you have to be able to motivate, inspire, mollycoddle, prod, annoy—whatever it takes to get that person to do what he or she is supposed to. There's never one set way to motivate someone. Different people have different buttons, different steerable points, and different ways of doing things.

On the other side of the coin—as a person being managed—I learned that success meant being the person who requires the least managing. It's what I teach my officers, my Marines, and the people I work with—if you are good at what you do, everything else will take care of itself.

I also learned how to be an effective decision maker under stress. In real time, you have to solve a problem while not causing other problems across the organization. There were no time-outs. There was no, "All you people waiting in line, would you please just go outside while we get our act together?"

People who have worked at McDonald's often talk about the crew like family and it's real. Until you've worked there, you don't realize what an incredible, intensive social experience it can be. We were proud to work there. People from the outside would give us a hard time: "Yeah, you work at McDonald's, the fast-food joint." And we'd say, "No. We work at *the* fast-food joint." Some of the best friends I have today are from my McDonald's years.

I was successful at McDonald's and could have stayed, but I enlisted in the Marine Corps Reserves. I went off to boot camp and was gone for about six or eight months. When I came back I started college and bounced in and out of school while being a full-time manager at McDonald's. I became a second assistant manager when I was twenty-two.

I really wanted to be a Marine Corps officer, so I left management and went back to being a swing manager, which is an hourly employee. I also delivered pizzas for Domino's for a while just to get my college degree, so I could then go to officer candidate school and move on. I appreciated the flexibility at McDonald's. It allowed me to do what I did.

I learned a lot about managing people from my time at McDonald's. Today, we call it mentoring or counseling—somebody takes an interest in another person and pulls them aside and says, "Hey, you screwed this up," or "Hey, you did really well today." It's not a formalized process of filling out forms. At McDonald's it was a very personalized experience. Because of that training, I figure if I have to tell somebody, "Hey, this is an order," then I've failed. In my twenty-six years in the Marine Corps, I've used that expression only once.

It took me about six years to get a four-year degree. I graduated from the University of Colorado in 1992 and headed to officer candidate school. From there I was commissioned as a second lieutenant and have been on active duty ever since.

I've had a successful career as a Marine. I've garnered several awards for leadership, the most significant of which was the Leftwich Trophy in 2001. The award is in memory of Lieutenant Colonel William Groom Leftwich, United States Marine Corps, who was killed in action in the Republic of Vietnam in November 1970. It's given each year to one outstanding Marine combat captain who is rated on things like line management, leadership, being able to read people, and inspiring others. Those are skills I first learned at McDonald's. I relearned them again the Marine Corps way, but I had already developed a pretty good foundation before that.

Today, I am a lieutenant colonel, commanding officer of a unit that's known as 1st Air Naval Gunfire Liaison Company, shortened to ANGLICO. Our mission is to provide fire and liaison expertise to joint allied and coalition forces that serve with Marine units. In Afghanistan we worked inside the battle space in Helmand province with Afghan National Army units, Canadians, Danes, Brits, United States Army units, and Special Operations forces. My unit was responsible for embedding with those units so that they could understand how the Marine Corps operates, but we were also a frontline fighting organization.

I am much more successful today than I would have been had I not worked at McDonald's. People ask me, and I tell them freely, "I learned a lot of lessons at McDonald's," which in my line of work raises a few eyebrows sometimes.

DID YOU KNOW?

1983: Hamburger University moved to its new home in Oak Brook, Illinois.
The first McDonald's in a railroad station opened in Philadelphia's Amtrak station.

Wendy Clark

AUTHOR'S NOTE

What someone takes away from a first job is often determined by what they bring to it. Wendy Clark was curious, driven, and competitive, and what she learned at McDonald's has served her well. Today, she is a senior marketing executive with The Coca-Cola Company in Atlanta, overseeing global design, content, media connections, and interactive marketing. She has twice been featured in *Fortune* magazine's 40 Under 40 profiles of up-and-coming executives and named one of its four Women to Watch. She says the most important lesson she learned at McDonald's was the secret to being a successful leader.

The biggest lesson I learned about being a good leader was that it's not about me, it's about the team.

When I went looking for my first real job to earn the money to buy my first car, there were plenty of restaurants to choose from at the end of the road where we lived in Sarasota,

Florida. McDonald's was viewed as a good, clean job for a sixteen-year-old. I knew my mother would have no qualms about her kid going to work there because I had cousins in Clearwater who worked at a McDonald's. I applied and the next thing I knew, I was wearing a blue uniform and visor.

I started as a crew member and loved it. Before long, my best friend had applied and was working there, too. I was determined to earn my money for the car I wanted to buy, but I also wanted experience and to learn everything I could. McDonald's used that in the most positive way, meeting my determination with opportunity and encouragement: "Here you go. Keep going."

One of my early successes was working the drive-thru. Because I lived in the UK until I was twelve—my father is British and my mother is American—I still had an accent. I'd just lay on the British accent and became so successful at up-selling that I won a state-level competition.

One of the techniques they used that motivated me was accumulating these pins they gave out when you became competent at a specific task. It was an outward symbol of success to stick on my hat, which quickly became festooned with pins. My driven personality worked well in a culture that encouraged learning new skills.

I was the first to raise my hand when they were looking for someone to volunteer for an assignment. That's how I ended up doing the kids' birthday parties. I had a background in day care and babysitting and loved children. I got to wear a little red vest, which I thought was really cool, and learned how to make a hamburger smile. (You take a bite, hold it up, and it's a smiley face.)

One of the tasks I was particularly proud of mastering was the shake machine. It had to be taken apart, cleaned, and put back together every single day. It required something like fifty steps, and I became one of just a handful of people who knew how to do it. Because I lived so close to the restaurant, they would often call me at home. "Can you come down and take the shake machine apart?" "Can you come in this morning and put it together?" Things like that made me feel valued.

At sixteen you don't realize the lessons you're learning—team dynamics, employee morale, customer service. You don't see the importance of those lessons. At that age, you're just having the raw experience.

Once I began to receive promotions, working there felt like being a member of a tribe. You could say that McDonald's is very much like a community. When you're with someone who is or has been part of the system, whether they are from Florida or Oregon, you immediately get a conversation going.

When I was promoted to swing-shift manager, I began to learn the lessons that influence how I operate today at The Coca-Cola Company, with a team of well over a hundred and responsibility for a budget in the millions. It's not easy to manage a diverse team with diverse backgrounds and the challenges that they're bringing in the door every day. The parallels between the Coca-Cola brand and the McDonald's brand are great. Whether it's in a single restaurant or a large enterprise, you have to deal simultaneously with customer satisfaction and employee morale.

During my time at McDonald's, I gained confidence in my ability to lead and motivate people. The biggest lesson about being a good leader was that it's not about me, it's about the team. The principle of coordinating a team now is the same as when I managed a shift. The less ego-based and arrogant a manager is and the more focused on the motivations of those being managed, the more success he or she will have. If a crew kid really doesn't want to be in the kitchen cooking, you had to figure out how to motivate that person to give their very best so that as a team you could succeed.

I like to say, "Lift as you climb." As you climb the ladder, you need to lift others. I also tell people all the time, "The more you give *it* away, the more of *it* you'll get." You can assign any meaning at all to the word *it*. If *it* is power, the more you give your power away, the more powerful you'll become. The more you make *it* about other people and take less credit for yourself, the more credit you'll get. That was a lesson I learned at McDonald's. The crew never wanted to work very hard for the managers who thought it was all about them. The managers who came in and put their people in the right places, really thought about the shift, and made it fun were the successful managers. They didn't come in saying, "I'm going to be successful." They came in and said, "We're going to be successful."

Those were all huge lessons and to learn them at age sixteen gave me a big head start.

DID YOU KNOW?

1985: McDonald's marks its thirtieth anniversary. The sausage McMuffin is added to the menu.

HIRED 1986

Stephanie Oliver-Green

AUTHOR'S NOTE

Second-generation McDonald's franchisees are becoming common, although fewer are minorities like Stephanie Oliver-Green, whose father bought his first restaurant in Chicago in 1979. Many of the things she talked about echoed what other owner/operators have said. What sets her apart are some unforgettable stories she shared about how she has used her position as a business woman and employer to help individuals who were down on their luck. "Mama," as she has come to be known, demonstrates in action the family feeling that so many people talk about when they recall their experiences. As disciplined as one has to be to work, manage, or own a McDonald's restaurant, Stephanie has taken risks and, in doing so, changed lives.

It's not about the burgers and fries anymore.
It's about changing and enriching people's lives.

I was nine years old in 1979 when my father bought his first restaurant in the Chicago area. He had been a basketball coach and a high school teacher. He knew a guy who owned some Burger King restaurants. There were not many African-American entrepreneurs owning businesses back then. My father is competitive by nature and said, "If he can own a Burger King, I'm going to look at owning a McDonald's." He had some land in Florida that he sold to get into the business.

That was thirty-three years ago, and today he and I own three McDonald's each in the Houston area, where we moved from Chicago in 1985. Growing up in my father's business, I had the chance to see him help many of the people he came into contact with. He changed some lives by getting them into the business. I've tried to live his example, and I could tell you fifty stories that would make you cry and send chills up your spine.

I think God has positioned me in the business of McDonald's to help people. So many people who need help talk to me and open up. Sometimes I ask, "Lord, why does everybody that You send to me have problems? Can't You send anybody here to help me?"

One of the people I'm proudest of is Tony (not his real name). He came to me at the age of eighteen. He was a runaway whose mother had died when he was twelve and was left with relatives who had molested him. He left that house and sought refuge in a church where he was molested again. So he ran away again, doing whatever he could to survive. He got caught writing hot checks and went to a juvenile facility. When I met him, he had just gotten out and came to one of our restaurants asking about a job.

At that time, I did all the hiring myself. The first time I set eyes on him, I didn't know how to approach him. He had on fake fingernails, so his hands looked like a lady's. Had he walked into a McDonald's in any other neighborhood, I doubt they'd have given him the time of day. But I've always had a soft spot for people, and I never look down on anyone. I feel like we're all equal, no matter what color, ethnicity, age, background, or walk of life.

So I just came out with it. "Come on now, baby. How are you going to work with these nails?"

He started laughing. "Oh, I'm sorry!" He hid his hands under the table.

I started going over his application, and there were a lot of questions he didn't answer about criminal background and convictions.

"You need to fill this out right here," I said, pointing.

He squirmed a bit and said, "Well, can I talk to you and tell you what happened about the conviction part?"

"Yeah."

"I really, really need this job. I don't know if you're going to hire me, but I just really, really need a new start and a change of life."

He started telling me his story, that he'd had a hard life and there was a lot he would like to share with me, but he was afraid that if he told me he wouldn't get the job. He didn't want me to feel like he was coming to work with a whole bunch of baggage and drama. But he was saying that if I could give him a second chance, I would never regret it and he would make me proud.

After a speech like that, what could I say?

"You know what? I don't even know you, but there's something about you. I'm going to give you a chance."

He burst into tears. That was something, for a young man to just sit in a McDonald's lobby and cry. Most males at that age are macho, and they don't want to look weak. But those nails!

"However," I said, "I'm going to have to work with you."

He turned out to be a good employee. It wasn't long after he began that he started calling me Mama. He'd clock in and greet me by saying, "Hey, Mama." People started thinking that he was my son. We looked nothing alike, but when he would say, "Mama," it was like he was really my child. I started getting compliments from customers. "Your son did a great job."

When he'd moved up to management and it was time for me to start helping the managers with life insurance, the woman who was collecting his information asked him, "Who are you going to put down for your beneficiary?"

He said, "My mama."

"Okay, what's your mama's name?"

"Stephanie Oliver-Green."

"Stephanie's your mama?"

You could not tell him that he was not my son. And if somebody were to tell him in the restaurant, "That's not your mama, quit playing," he would get defensive. He would say, "That's the only mother I know who's been there for me."

It took something like a mother's love when I had to send Tony to jail.

He would come to me sometimes to ask me for money for his rent. I would always loan it to him, and he always paid it back. One day one of my employees responsible for bookkeeping came to me and said there was a discrepancy between a bank deposit Tony had made and how much it should have been. Money was missing. I did the hard thing and called the police to report him. Then I asked him about it, and he was honest.

"Yeah, Mama, I did it."

"Why would you do that? You can ask me for anything. I will give you the shirt off my back. You don't have to steal from me."

He said he felt tired of always asking me for money, and he was going to put it back before I ever noticed it was missing.

"You don't have the authority to make your own loans in the restaurant without letting me know. I'm sorry, but I've called the police and made a report because it's theft."

"I know," he said. "Whatever you have to do, I'm going to confess to it."

Sure enough, the police picked him up, and he spent some weeks in jail. When he came out, he apologized again, paid the money back, told me he loved me, and promised he would never do it again.

I hired him back, I loved him that much. If it was my kid, I'd do the same thing: "You're going to be accountable for what you did. I'm going to teach you. And I'm going to whip you with love."

I haven't had a problem since. He's one of my first assistant managers. It's been twelve years since he came to me, and he's still calling me Mama.

Another person who touched my life is a girl named Rachel (also not a real name). She first came to me about ten years ago and worked at one of the restaurants. I didn't understand what was going on with her, but everybody would always tell me, "Rachel wants to be just like you."

When I'd come to work and announce, "Mama's here," she'd say, "Little Mama's here." Everything I did she mimicked.

I noticed that every month she had a new boyfriend. Her mother had died of a drug overdose and she had a son, but she wasn't spending a lot of time with him. I tried to get to know more about her.

Along the way, she ended up getting into drugs. She went to rehab, and I was there with her almost every day, praying with her and telling her that she's a beautiful person. I stayed on the phone with her and spent hours building her back up. She was so torn down and had been going back and forth with these men who abused her.

I'm very proud to say that she still works for me too, even though she went back to school and got a pharmacist degree. She was one of my top salaried managers, and although she went ahead making more money at a pharmacy, she told me that she still felt loyal and committed to me. She would always work with me part time because she just doesn't want to leave. McDonald's is home to her.

As an owner/operator or as a manager, you need to dig deep into people's lives, know your people, and be in tune with what's going on. The people that work for you may have struggles you know nothing about. For example, there was an older Spanish-speaking lady, Rosa (not her real name), who worked at one of my locations. One night my manager called me and said, "Miss Stephanie, I just want to let you know Rosa is gone. She's fired. She's been stealing granola." The granola comes in little packets and goes on the parfaits.

I said, "Come on! For real? We're going to fire her over some granola?"

She said, "Miss Stephanie, she had a whole bag of the packets."

I asked myself, "What the heck could she be doing with some granola?"

I wanted to talk to her, but I knew she only spoke a little bit of English, so I had to get a different manager who could translate. We got Rosa on the phone.

I told the manager, "Find out why she would take the granola. What is she trying to do?"

Rosa was sobbing uncontrollably. She didn't want to say why. She said she'd give it back and was sorry. She said she wouldn't work at McDonald's anymore and please forgive her.

I said, "No, no, no. That's not important. I want to know why she is taking the granola. What's wrong?"

Finally, after about thirty minutes crying on the phone, she told us that her husband had left her and she didn't have any money. Her kids didn't have anything to eat. She got paid on the fifth and the twentieth of the month. It was about the seventeenth, so she was taking that granola home to mix with water and make cereal until she got her check.

I said, "Tell Rosa to clock back in and go to work. I'll see her tomorrow, and I'm going to give her fifty dollars to buy some groceries."

A lot of people don't realize that McDonald's is the land of opportunity for a lot of folks. I feel it's the responsibility of African Americans who've been blessed with a franchise to talk to our communities and let them know about our brand and the opportunities McDonald's can offer them. Nobody can tell our story like we can. When I go speak at high schools and let them know I own a McDonald's in the area, those kids are blown away.

I'm very proud to be in the position I'm in. To me, it's not about the burgers and fries anymore. It's about changing and enriching people's lives.

DID YOU KNOW?

1986: McDonald's introduced three varieties of biscuit sandwiches.

HIRED 1989

Kyong Kapalczynski

AUTHOR'S NOTE

The most profound lesson I have learned in my career is the importance of helping others achieve their dreams. One of the success stories I am most proud to have helped facilitate is the career of Kyong Kapalczynski, a South Korean woman who came to America as the wife of an American soldier. She knew very little English. Her first American meal was a McDonald's cheeseburger and she decided that's where she wanted to work. When I met her, she was struggling to make the leap from restaurant manager to owner/operator. Her journey is the story of so many new Americans who cope with language, prejudice, and economic challenges, yet manage to flourish in the fertile soil of American capitalism.

I'm going to show them what I can do.

South Korea is my homeland but I was enamored with America and when my husband asked me to marry him, I had no trouble saying yes. In 1989 the Army reassigned him stateside and we moved with our two little girls to Frederick, Maryland. On a stopover in Seattle to visit one of my uncles, we popped into a McDonald's on the way into town from the airport. It was the first American meal I ate.

I had never eaten anything as good as a McDonald's cheeseburger. I could have eaten three or four. I decided right then that McDonald's would be the first place I looked for a job when the kids started school. I found a restaurant that was a twenty-minute walk from our apartment, which was convenient because I hadn't yet learned how to drive. I started out on the opening shift

My English wasn't the best, so I was very shy about speaking. I just applied with a smile, and they hired me.

Within six months, my manager put me into the company's management development program. My husband helped me study the materials, and I was promoted to swing manager and then to kitchen-area manager. But just as I was completing my course work, my husband, an army recruiting officer, was reassigned again, to his home state of Montana. We would have to move right away. I burst into tears when I heard the news. I had worked so hard to get to my position at work and I was upset at having to give it up and start over somewhere else.

As soon as we had moved to Montana, I applied at the local McDonald's. As I was filling out the application, I looked around and realized that it was not at all like Maryland. I heard nothing for a week so I went back and put in a second application. Still nobody called.

My husband decided it was time to get involved so, in his uniform, he went with me on my third visit. "We would like to speak to the owner," I told the boy at the counter. The owner came out from the back and I explained that I had worked at a company-owned restaurant in Maryland, had completed my training studies, and had just gotten a manager position when we had to move.

"So can you hire me? I don't mind if I have to go back as a crew member."

He agreed and I was back at work. I was so happy to be back in McDonald's, and I told myself, I'm going to show them what I can do.

My first year or two working in the States were very hard and I did shed a few tears. When you don't speak English well and you are different, people tend to pick on you and give you the worst jobs. But I did them, did them all the way, and then did extra work. I wanted to show them who I am, that I can do it, even though I'm a different skin color. I wanted them to see me, how hard I worked.

I even volunteered for all the jobs nobody else wanted to do—sweeping, mopping, cleaning the bathrooms. I would sweep sometimes seven or eight times during my shift because I like to work in a clean place and do a great job. I was never late and never called in sick. This was my culture. Calling in sick in Asian cultures is shameful because you're making everybody else work harder.

I worked as many hours as I could. Being paid hourly was motivating me because in Korea employees are paid by the month no matter how many hours they work. In the States, I had the chance to make more money—an opportunity to get ahead.

When I had gotten all the hours I could at McDonald's, I took a second job as a nurse's aide in an old-age facility. They paid more than McDonald's but the work wasn't for me. It was very slow paced and I liked the busy-ness of McDonald's. Also I became attached to the patients, and then they'd pass away. I got so emotional I couldn't sleep.

After about two years in Montana, the owner of the McDonald's where I worked offered me the chance to resume the courses I had taken in Maryland and get back onto the management track. I attended a training class in the state of Washington where one of the teachers helped me with my English and explained the questions on the exams. I managed to pass the tests and was certified as a swing manager.

Then it happened again. My husband was transferred, this time to Oregon. I had to go start over again.

In Oregon I was hired at a McDonald's as a swing manager. Soon I was promoted to assistant manager and then manager. I earned progress awards, and the restaurant owner gave me bonuses when my sales rose. He also gave me the chance to take the highest level of management courses at Hamburger University in suburban Chicago.

One day the regional manager for the Northwest Region came to visit, which was exciting. I proudly showed her the awards and citations I had received, including the Ray Kroc award, which is given to only the top 1 percent of restaurant managers in the country. I told her that my dream was to own my own restaurant someday.

"You're doing a great job," she said. "Yes, you can do it." She gave me such hope. That person was Cody Teets, the author of this book.

The requirements for purchasing a McDonald's restaurant are high. To own one you must have experience working on the operational side of the restaurant business. In a company of this size with a reputation to maintain, who represents you to your customers is important. Owners are also expected to have substantial cash or liquid assets.

My husband had retired from military service and he had owned another quick-service restaurant for two years. He knew the profit potential was good, so we decided to empty out all our piggy banks and see if we could raise the capital. We sold our house and moved into a small two-bedroom apartment. My husband sold his beloved hockey and baseball card collections. We sold everything, and then the rules were that I had to quit McDonald's while my application was being considered.

During the waiting time, we were really poor. I needed a job and there wasn't much available. I asked the landlord where we lived if he had any work, and he hired me to clean apartments after tenants had moved out. I vacuumed carpets and swabbed toilets for a year or so while we waited.

Finally, an opportunity opened up and we were able to purchase a restaurant in Oregon. We owned it for about two years when we were offered several McDonald's in Montana, where I had worked and where my husband grew up.

Today we own all four McDonald's in Missoula, and the chances are one in four that if you walked into any of them, you would find me out front taking orders, or working the grill, or maybe even cleaning the bathroom. In spite of the cultural divide and the language barrier, I am living the American dream.

The most important thing that I learned about being in business from my early days working at McDonald's is how to manage people with many different backgrounds and personalities. For example, let's say you have two managers who need to be corrected. One has a high temper and one is very laid back. I cannot use the same approach with two different personalities. The high-tempered one I have to calm down and be firmer with than the other one.

I tell people who work for me, "Right now you might not make what you want, but in the future, there is opportunity. Let's do baby steps and see how it works. If you're willing to follow me, I'm willing to help you to grow."

Because I work in my restaurants, I am sometimes spotted by Asian tourists who stop in on their way to Yellowstone Park. They look at me in surprise, and sometimes I say hello to them and tell them who I am. They ask me why I am in Montana. I tell them "I love it here. Before, I was shy. Now, I'm the boss. In America if you do well, it doesn't matter what state you live in."

DID YOU KNOW?

1989: The McChicken Sandwich was rolled out nationally after ten years of testing.

1990s

HIRED 1991

Jerry W. Hairston, Jr.

AUTHOR'S NOTE

As a family business, professional baseball is among the more unusual. Within professional baseball, the Hairstons are considered the largest family, with the most members to have played in the major and minor leagues. Jerry Hairston, Jr.'s, grandfather, father, brother, and uncle have all been professionals, giving Jerry Jr. the additional distinction of being the first African-American to be a third generation major-leaguer. His father insisted he get a job and experience what it's like to work hard. That's how Jerry ended up at a McDonald's, where he learned a couple of lessons that helped him in his career.

No matter what you want to do in life,
you've got put all your effort into it.

My dad grew up in a very different time—the 1950s and 1960s, in Birmingham, Alabama, during the height of the civil rights movement. He was the first black student at Gardendale

High School in the Birmingham suburbs in the 1960s and had to work hard for everything from an early age. He had a successful career in baseball, so our family was financially secure. When I was a teenager, he pushed me to get a job. He wanted to instill a good work ethic in me and make sure I understood the value of hard work.

McDonald's had just opened a new restaurant down the street from where we lived in Naperville, Illinois, and they were hiring. It was the perfect job for me because it was convenient and they were able to give me hours that didn't conflict with school and sports. I worked there for six months until my practice and class schedules made it impossible to continue, but I learned a lot in that short time that I still can relate to in my career.

Working at McDonald's taught me about accountability. Our restaurant was always busy, so you had to be on top of things and think ahead. I had to be prepared and felt pressure not to slack off because the other crew members were relying on me. When you make the French fries, for example, you need to make sure there are enough to meet the demand. I had to be on top of my game, no matter what.

The same thing applies in my baseball career. People are counting on me to do my best—my teammates, the city, and the people who pay to see me play and support their team. Now I'm going on my fifteenth year in the major leagues, so I guess my dad got his point across. When I came home tired from a shift at the restaurant, he seemed pleased when I'd say, "Work was hard today!"

Working at McDonald's was an eye-opening experience because I was exposed to an incredibly diverse group of people of different ages and backgrounds. In sports and in school, everyone was around the same age and came from a similar upbringing. I remember noticing that everybody on crew was equally industrious, no matter what their background. I gained their respect and trust by sharing their work ethic and the goal of serving customers.

My McDonald's job taught me the value of responsibility as it was the first time I worked for a paycheck and learned the value of money. I had my allowance before that, but there's nothing like making your own money and realizing the importance of saving. I knew what it had taken to earn every penny, so I tried to spend it wisely. That was huge.

The biggest thing about the job was that it made me take a step back, set goals, and think about my future. I knew I wanted to be a professional baseball player like my dad, uncle, and grandfather. My job gave me perspective, teaching me the connection between making a commitment and sticking with it and achieving my goals. No matter what you want to do in life, you've got to put all your effort into it.

Being a crew member taught me lessons I rely upon to this day.

DID YOU KNOW?

The Hairstons are one of only three families
to have had three generations of
major league baseball players.

HIRED 1992

Alma Anguiano

AUTHOR'S NOTE

Alma Anguiano's story is one of the most dramatic in this collection—she entered the US as an infant from Mexico; grew up in a neighborhood of Los Angeles that was so rough she was afraid to go to school; became the first in her large family to earn a college degree; and is today a successful human resources executive with McDonald's in California, working with the owner/operators of more than 550 restaurants. Her incredible journey is an affirmation of the American dream and an inspiration to those who strive to achieve it. It's also the portrait of a young girl who learned to become a leader in her family before she was even an adult.

Life is full of roadblocks. The challenge is figuring out how to clear those roadblocks, but there is always a way.

any people come to America speaking no English. I arrived before I had learned to speak at all, an infant and the first child of Mexican parents. Our family settled in Los Angeles where my mother found work as a seamstress and my father worked in a cardboard box factory. No one in our family spoke English, so when I started to learn it in kindergarten, I became the family's translator, deciphering important papers and other documents as best I could. It was a double challenge because my Spanish vocabulary was limited, especially in writing. When I was later placed in a Spanish class to learn how to read and write in my native language, I quickly became a bilingual reader.

In fifth grade, one of the sixth-grade teachers—Mrs. Washington—took an interest in me and enrolled me in her magnet class. She took me under her wing, even teaching me the proper use of a fork and knife—at home we mostly used tortillas to pick up our food. She put a road map together for my education—the schools I needed to go to, the steps I needed to take—so that I could go to college. That's when I realized I could make something of myself.

Being the oldest of six, I shared responsibility for my four brothers and one sister When I started earning some cash working at a swap meet, I saved up enough to buy all the kids coats one Christmas.

For the first fourteen years of my life we lived in Los Angeles in a rundown neighborhood controlled by gangs. My brothers were often harassed, and my sister kept getting into fights. I was sure my brothers would end up in gangs, my sister would end up with the wrong boyfriend, and I didn't know what would become of me. I was determined either to go to Mexico and live with my grandparents or move away to a better area to live with one of my relatives so I could continue school.

We still lived in a bad neighborhood when I started ninth grade. I was terrified of going to school. The high school was in Watts, a neighborhood that became infamous in the 1960s for the riots that occurred there. My first day in class was also the teacher's first day, and the students hid all of his things.

The kids were intimidating, wanting to know what gang I was in, so I stopped going to school.

For an entire semester, while my parents were working and thought

I was in class, I stayed home and cleaned and read my textbooks. Finally, the school sent home a notice, and I told my parents I wanted to move to Mexico. Instead, we all decided to move to Dinuba, a lovely little farm town in California's Central Valley where I had a cousin.

The catalyst for my career was the manager of the local McDonald's—Nancy Korsak—who came to speak at our high school. I was feeling guilty at the time because the move from Watts, which was for my benefit, meant my parents were having trouble finding new jobs. The family was struggling to make ends meet. When Nancy finished her talk, I went up to her and said, "I really need a job. Will you hire me?"

"Go to the restaurant," she said, "and write on the application that you met me here."

When I got to McDonald's, I discovered I wasn't the only one inspired by her talk—they already had a stack of applications. My peers in that agricultural region thought it was cool, even prestigious, to work at McDonald's or Kmart or any sort of retail setting. It meant you didn't have to work in the fields picking crops or in the packing houses like most other kids.

I filled my application out and decided I would wait as long as it took to speak to Nancy when she came in. I was nervous at first, but as I sat there studying the bustling crew, I began to think, *I can do that. I can take orders, and I think I can work in the kitchen, too.* I was trying to figure out what I should say when Nancy walked in.

I presented myself. "Remember me?"

She looked at her watch. "Oh, my goodness! You waited for me for three hours?" And that's how I got the job, and how Nancy became my mentor and played a big role in my life and career.

I threw myself into the work, staying after my shifts ended to volunteer and learn as much as I could as fast as I could. After four months, I knew that restaurant inside and out, from opening to closing. Being the oldest child of six and having as much responsibility as I did growing up was helpful. Leadership seemed to come naturally to me.

The owner/operators, Mark and Rosanna Ruiz, also looked out for me. When I became a full-time employee in my senior year of high school, they encouraged me to finish school and keep my sights on attending college. When I turned nineteen, they sold their restaurant and asked me to come along to their new restaurant in Sacramento as a manager. It meant I had to move away from home for the first time in my life. I didn't get to go home much because it was a three-and-a-half-hour trip, and I was always busy.

My parents were happy because I sent them money every month, but they still had the dream for me to graduate from college. What they said is funny in retrospect. "We don't want you to stop going to school because we want you to *be* something, like a teacher." Yet there I was, nineteen years old and running a business with an annual revenue of more than $2 million.

Everybody in my family started moving to Sacramento, and I think all my siblings worked for McDonald's at one point or another. My oldest brother is now a restaurant manager for Panera Bread. It took me ten years, but I did finally earn my bachelor's degree in business administration. Mark and Rosanna even helped pay for my books, as long as I kept my grades up.

I learned so much as a young person working at McDonald's, but the most important lesson is that everything is possible. Life is full of roadblocks. The challenge is figuring out how to clear those roadblocks, but there is always a way. I've applied that lesson in every aspect of my life.

One of the hardest lessons I've had to learn as an adult is how to balance life and work. And I've had to learn to accept that not everyone wants to make McDonald's their life career. When people I have trained decide to take a different path, it sometimes feels a little like I've failed. I've learned that if I want something for a person more than they do, that's a problem. Often when I look at young kids at the restaurant, I can see their potential. I know they could be so much more than they are, but they don't necessarily want to hear it.

Today, I'm director of human resources for the company's Pacific Sierra Region, helping the owner/operators of close to 560 restaurants with strategy and regulatory issues. My parents are very proud, but they express it in different ways. My mother will say things like, "If it wasn't for you, God knows where we would be." My father is a man of few words.

He doesn't express his feelings directly, probably because compliments embarrass me. Instead he brags behind my back. One day my brother called me and said, "Dad could not stop talking about you with his friend, about what you've done and where you're at."

In my current position I am often in our restaurants talking to managers. Every time I walk into a McDonald's, I remember that day twenty years ago when I sat in a chair in Dinuba, studying the crew and waiting for Nancy, dreaming of a future that has come true.

DID YOU KNOW?

1992: McDonald's introduced the advertising slogan, "What You Want Is What You Get."

Karen Wells

AUTHOR'S NOTE

While almost all the people profiled here first encountered McDonald's as teens, there are those who come to work for the company as adults with professional experience elsewhere. For those of us who have been on the inside looking out most of our lives, it's interesting to hear how their experiences differ from their expectations. Karen Wells thought she knew what McDonald's was all about when she came calling as a potential vendor. Instead of a sale, she walked away with a job that led to playing a pivotal role in one the company's most important initiatives and the chance to work with the White House and First Lady Michelle Obama.

As big as McDonald's is, you get a feeling that it's a very large family.

As a teenager, I never would have dreamed of working at McDonald's, even though I liked the food. I had bought into the notion that flipping burgers was beneath my capabilities, even though I had a similar entry-level job as a clerk in a retail store. In my youthful mind, the two were unequal.

My attitude reflected in part my ambition. I grew up in a family of ten children with parents who divorced early in my life. I spent part of my youth in North Carolina with my mother and part in Ohio with my father, who had a career in the military. Making ends meet was often a challenge and my experiences motivated me to get educated so I could land a good job.

Graduating from college with a marketing degree, I initially found work as a buyer for the Drackett Company, a maker of household products such as Windex, Drano, and Renuzit. Then I worked in sales for M&M-Mars Candy Company. It occurred to me one day that it would be quite a coup to sell our products to a large company like McDonald's. They didn't sell candy bars, but they did sell ice cream, and my company made crushed candies that could be mixed into ice cream. Had I known what a long shot that was, I might have considered it a waste of time and missed out on the opportunity of a lifetime.

I made a cold call to a regional purchasing manager in Raleigh, North Carolina, named Betsy Gaona. Knowing what I know today, Betsy could have been excused for saving herself some time by turning me down flat. Instead, she was friendly and welcoming. She agreed to have me make a presentation to her purchasing committee without being prescreened. I was excited to try and land a new account, and a potentially big one.

After the presentation I waited hopefully for news. The call came and the answer was, "No, but… "

"No on the Snickers bars, but we'd like you to come and interview for a job."

The position was in my chosen field, marketing, and it was a good situation—regional marketing supervisor in one of the forty regions McDonald's had in the US at the time. I didn't hesitate to say yes. I figured it would be an office job and, if nothing else, a ticket out of sales.

When I got started, I was a little baffled by the high morale, pride, and self-confidence expressed by the staff. They seemed to love what they did. I thought, It's just McDonald's. It's just a hamburger. What's the big deal?

What I came to discover, as many had before me and have since, is that it's actually a fun and well-run place to work, and it has made a lot of people financially comfortable.

One of my first impressions was how much work goes into making it look easy. I was responsible for presenting to the franchisees in one TV market the company's national marketing plans. In almost every case, the owner/operators had to vote to approve what we were proposing. My job was one of influence, being able to present convincingly and then fielding tough questions, like how much would a particular marketing program cost the owner/operators or how would a particular promotion affect their operations. My role was to present a compelling case on why this promotion was a good business decision and how the plan could be executed in a way that allowed the restaurants to maintain their service and product standards, while at the same time make money.

It was an eye-opener to learn that 85 percent of the system is run by independent owner/operators—small-business people who may have swapped a previous career to have a family business. Some of the most successful ideas at the company started out with an idea from a franchisee. The Big Mac and Egg McMuffin are prime examples.

The other eye-opening thing was how assertively McDonald's promotes from within. Five years after I started as a marketing manager, some people who had taken me under their wings said, "We see potential in you and think you could go into operations." It was a challenge and an opportunity that I welcomed.

Three years later, I was an operations director responsible for 450 restaurants. Within three years of becoming a director, I became an officer of the company, starting first in the Indianapolis region and then moving on to manage a department in strategy, innovation, and menu.

Ultimately I became responsible for a cross-discipline team—from operations to marketing to nutrition and food scientists—that runs all of the food innovation for the US business and the 26 million people we feed each day. My career feels like a phenomenon to me, especially as an African American. I don't know if I could name another company that could deliver such opportunities to grow, to try new things, to be always learning. No two days are the same.

Turns out, it's quite a bit more than just a hamburger.

My most treasured experience with the company came out of our efforts to evolve our Happy Meals to meet the changing preferences of customers. I was given the assignment to lead the development of our nutrition platform for McDonald's USA. Working with our government relations experts, we organized a partnership with First Lady Michelle Obama on a child-obesity initiative called "Let's Move." There were many meetings and discussions at the White House and at the company's headquarters in Oakbrook, Illinois. I had the privilege of getting to meet Mrs. Obama, who helped win support from the nutrition community.

I recently celebrated twenty years with McDonald's and stepped down from my position leading the US menu team to work part time so I can be more involved with our two school-age children. I've been traveling all their lives. In this sense, as big as McDonald's is, you do get a feeling that it's a very large family.

When McDonald's people get together, one of the things that often happens is people will ask, "What's your 'I' story?" That's the story about how you came to work for the company and your experiences since. "I started in a restaurant," or "I started out in marketing, and now I'm in operations," or "I started in the field, and now I'm in the home office." Everyone has an "I" story, and it's a great icebreaker. My "I" story begins with an unfounded prejudice—I would never dream of flipping burgers.

Today, I would have no qualms about my kids working at McDonald's because I know now that it's hard, honest work, a great experience, and rich with opportunities. Since my candy presentation that became a job offer, my sister has become a restaurant manager and my nieces and nephews have started at McDonald's, too. It's clearly become a family business for us.

DID YOU KNOW?

1992: Baked apple pies replaced fried apple pies on the menu.

Travis Heriaud

AUTHOR'S NOTE

Almost a third of the people who own and operate McDonald's restaurants today are second-generation franchisees, up from 18 percent in 2001. That number is expected to continue rising as baby boomers retire. This trend was the subject of a front page *Wall Street Journal* article in March 2012 about how the next generation is reinvigorating the company. Among those featured were Travis Heriaud and his father, Lee, who own twelve restaurants in the Phoenix area. Although he was the son of an owner, Travis had to go through the same rigorous multi-year process as anyone else does to be approved as a franchisee. One of his most interesting observations is that young people's perceptions of working in a quick-service restaurant like McDonald's are much more positive than you'd expect.

Being a franchisee is like being a small-business owner but at the same time being part of a global brand.

Although my official hire date is in 1995, I really began working in a McDonald's in 1988, when I was about seven. I was barely tall enough to reach the tops of the tables. My father would take me with him to work, and I'd go around with a wet towel and wipe everything down.

I loved going to work with my father. He was an enthusiastic owner/operator who had started out when he was fourteen years old at McDonald's in Naperville, Illinois. He was one of fourteen children who grew up on a rented farm in a two-bedroom house with no plumbing or electricity. Before McDonald's, he worked beside his siblings in the fields before and after school. McDonald's made it possible for him to go to college and help support his family.

Under the guidance of owner/operator Gus Kapellas, my father rose to second-in-command of five restaurants. When Gus wanted to move to Arizona, he sold his five restaurants in Illinois, bought five restaurants in Arizona, and my father went with him. Then he became an owner/operator himself in 1989 when he bought restaurants from Gus.

As much as I begged, my father wouldn't let me go to work in his restaurants until I was fourteen. After that I worked there every summer. My father's mantra was education first, so I wasn't allowed to work during the school year. He also insisted I get a college degree, which I did. But I flew home during breaks my first year just to work. I inherited my father's enthusiasm for the business and wanted to be a franchisee one day, too.

My dad always delegated the job of being my boss to someone else, but if I did something he disapproved of I heard about it. One day I woke up vomiting and sick as a dog. I just stayed in bed and didn't call in that day. I got a huge lecture for that.

In spite of what most people think, when your dad owns a McDonald's, it isn't just handed to you. That was fine with me. I welcomed the challenge. When I started the process for being approved to be a franchisee, I told my father, "I do not believe in entitlement. I want you to make it as hard as you possibly can, because otherwise I won't deserve what comes with it."

Part of what drives me is the desire to make my dad proud.

It's been interesting to see how perceptions of McDonald's, my own and those of others, have evolved over the years. When I was a kid, the fact that my dad worked for McDonald's made me an instant legend on the playground. When I was a teenager, it hit me that maybe it wasn't that cool anymore. Then one day my friends from high school showed up at work.

My first thought was that they would say something disparaging or embarrassing. Instead they said, "Oh, my God! This is so cool. You get to do whatever you want back there?" One of my buddies tried to walk behind the counter to see, and I had to stop him. "Hey, I'm glad you think this is cool, but you can't come behind here." It was not what I expected at all.

Many of the kids who come to work at McDonald's start out with a low opinion of their new employer. Then when they realize the opportunities, a light goes on and they feel pride.

Today I spend a lot of time volunteering and teaching high school students, and it's always interesting to hear what they truly feel about the brand. Many times I've heard teens express in one way or another that they're *supposed* to be skeptical about McDonald's. That's what they get from the culture or their parents. But what they really feel is often quite different. They enjoy the food, and they express genuine respect for what the owner/operators and the company do for their communities.

What I enjoy about being a franchisee is that it's like being a small-business owner, running your own profit-and-loss statements and doing your own hires, but at the same time you're part of a global brand. If I were to work for a corporation, I would have my specific function within the corporation. But to own a McDonald's means I get to do everything.

Our company has over 700 employees. I work directly with the managers and interact with our regular customers. I work with key company marketing experts and owner/operators to design marketing and brand initiatives for the upcoming year. In addition to influencing my restaurants, my teams, and my community, I'm also able to work collaboratively in designing the future for 14,000 restaurants.

How many businesses can you be in where you're involved in

marketing, finance, real estate, and you also get to help develop your own people so their dreams come true too?

DID YOU KNOW?

1995: McDonald's launched its "Have You Had Your Break Today" advertising slogan.

HIRED 1997

Charles L. Broughton

AUTHOR'S NOTE

The perception that working at McDonald's requires little skill and is a dead-end job has been a deeply personal issue for Charles Broughton. As a child and young adult, he often felt he had to defend the fact that his father worked for McDonald's, even when he was a supervisor and later a director of operations. Charles grew up in the business but still had to establish his own credentials, which he did while still in his twenties. Today, not quite thirty years old, he is a supervisor responsible for six restaurants in Massachusetts. He has been a Ray Kroc Award winner, an honor earned each year by the top 1 percent of the system's 14,000 restaurant managers. He has also established himself as a change agent by introducing an innovative marketing idea that caught the attention of senior management.

I could go work in any industry in any business and succeed just because of the skills and the foundation that McDonald's has taught me.

I've been around McDonald's my entire life. When I was young and told other kids what my dad did, the reaction was often, "Oh, so your dad just flips burgers." It was embarrassing because I didn't understand. I remember constantly feeling I had to defend his job. I was so proud of him and knew he had an important position, but it was hard because everyone just assumed he was a crew person. Now that I'm older and I understand the industry, it's become a passion of mine to change people's perceptions.

My dad got started at McDonald's about thirty-five years ago, in his twenties. He was teaching junior high school and got a job at McDonald's over the summer as breakfast coordinator. Eventually he decided to leave teaching and work just for McDonald's, right around the time I was born. His family and friends thought he was crazy. "Why would you leave such a stable job in education to go to McDonald's?" Thirty years later, he's a director of operations for a group of thirteen restaurants and very successful.

In the early nineties, my dad worked for an owner/operator as a supervisor of about ten restaurants. When I was seven or eight years old, my father started taking me with him on Saturdays and putting me to work, standing on a milk crate to prepare hash browns or being an extra set of hands for the maintenance man.

I officially started at McDonald's when I was fourteen. My intention was to make some money to buy video games and things like that. When I was a year or two older and gaining a better understanding of the business, my dad started taking me with him to meetings and conventions. I got to see the business end of McDonald's early on—the upper management and what goes on at these meetings. It opened my eyes to how I was becoming part of something that was so much bigger. I began to view myself as working in a family business.

I continued working at McDonald's full time while I was in college. By then, I was running shifts and closing the restaurant. In college I wasn't sure whether I was going to stick with McDonald's. I've always been interested in marketing, specifically advertising, and that's the route I was hoping to go.

Within the first three or four months after I graduated college, in 2005, I got a couple of offers to work at marketing firms. I also got an offer from my boss to be a McDonald's restaurant manager. It was an easy decision—I could use my marketing skills in a business I already knew well.

One of the things few people know about McDonald's is that it sends many employees to classes that teach business concepts and skills, including some you don't learn in college. For someone who doesn't have the opportunity to go to college, these classes are a tremendous opportunity. My main argument for staying at McDonald's is that from there I could go work in many industries and succeed largely because of the skills and the foundation that McDonald's has taught me.

Whether it's for a summer or a career, we teach people about business: how to run one, what the inner workings are like, how to be professional. I don't think the public understands all that we do for our employees. It's like a shape-up opportunity to learn what it means to be on time, to dress properly, and so on. Those are habits our younger crew people learn that will last a lifetime.

Today, I am an area supervisor, responsible for six restaurants in Massachusetts. When I tell someone what I do for a living and they give me the burger-flipper response, I point out that I'm on par with my high school friends both financially and professionally. Currently I'm responsible for 200 employees and over $15 million of sales.

I'm proud of my career but even prouder of the number of people I helped groomed as assistant managers who have now moved up the ranks.

The thing that really put me on the map within the company was a marketing idea I had that we called Customer Appreciation Day. This was in a restaurant in a small town where we have a lot of regular customers. In a lot of places McDonald's is the local café. You see the same people there every day. They meet for their coffee and spend several hours there. They get to know all our names and we know theirs. As soon as they walk in the door, we can prepare their coffee without them having to order.

I was looking for some kind of spark that was different. The idea I had was a day when we allowed customers to go behind the counter and make their own drinks and get a tour of the restaurant. The idea for Customer Appreciation Day was in conjunction with the rollout of McCafé. Customers liked having an opportunity to see what exactly was going on behind the counters when they placed an order, to see us cracking the eggs to make the McMuffins. We had a lot of traffic and excitement.

McDonald's executives came to observe. That's what really first got my name out there with the corporation and with McDonald's in general. It surprises people to learn that an individual manager can come up with an idea or a product that could one day be used across the whole system. The Big Mac, Egg McMuffin, and Filet-O-Fish are good examples of ideas that came directly from employees. We've done a second Customer Appreciation Day and are hoping to do it again in the future.

I know McDonald's is a huge corporation, but I like that it still feels like I'm working in a family business.

DID YOU KNOW?

1997: There are more than 23,000 McDonald's restaurants open around the globe.

2000s

HIRED 2002

Majasyn Turner

AUTHOR'S NOTE

If you're the parent of a twenty-five-year-old who's sitting at home out of work, Majasyn Turner's story will probably make you blush. This twenty-five-year-old manages four busy restaurants with over 200 employees and more than $10 million in annual sales. She has been ranked in the top one percent of all McDonald's USA managers. If you are the parent of a sixteen-year-old who is overwhelmed by her first job, you will want to make sure she reads Majasyn's story because she was overwhelmed by hers, too. How did she get from there to where she is today? Among other skills, she supervises with empathy, a quality that companies increasingly recognize makes for great leaders and one that has served her well.

It isn't all about the numbers,
it's also about what you bring to the table.

Growing up, I worked in my mother's day care business. Keeping track of all those kids and making sure they were safe and comfortable may have been good training for later on in my career, but McDonald's was my first real job and a big shock.

I was sixteen, and they put me on French fries my first day. It was Friday, a busy day. There were so many people to interact with and so much going on. The person in charge showed me the equipment and said, "Here's how to do the fries. You drop the fries, and you bag them up. That's all." A little later, a shift manager walked by and scolded me for doing it wrong and falling behind on the orders.

That first night, on my way home from McDonald's in Ontario, California, I was discouraged. "This is really not for me," I thought. "What am I going to do?" But I come from a family of athletes and had a lot of positive role models. I knew I'd have to go back and try again.

My first-day experience was helpful to me later on. I learned that to get along with so many different personality types, I had to accept that everyone learns and works in different ways. Some people are visual and some prefer to read instructions. I've learned to accept everybody for who they are.

Today, I tell my managers to find the best job for each person. I make sure people feel comfortable with their jobs because I remember how overwhelmed I felt on my first day. I stuck it out, got comfortable in the restaurant, and soon my coworkers felt like family.

One day Kiana Webb-Severloh, the daughter of the owner/operator and going through the steps to becoming an owner/operator herself, asked if I would like to become a crew trainer, responsible for training new hires. I would be attending classes to learn all the stations, and I'd get a raise. I was surprised because I had only been there about eight months. It made me happy that she pushed me to do more. I went home and excitedly told my parents, who beamed with pride.

As a crew trainer, I discovered a natural ability to lead, which I had developed bossing my younger sister around and helping with Mom's day care business. I caught on quickly and was willing to learn new things. I had no idea about staying at McDonald's, but I figured I should make the best of it while I was there.

My biggest challenge was my age. Many of the trainees were older than me. Within a year, when I was seventeen, I was promoted to shift manager. I had to take a test and was nervous, so I didn't do so well. But the director of operations passed me anyway, saying, "You had a great attitude, and that tells me you'll be trainable." That was another learning experience—it isn't all about the numbers, it's also about what you bring to the table.

When I graduated from high school, I went to a culinary arts school while still working at McDonald's. In addition to learning how to cook, which I love, I learned a lot about the business of restaurants, like food costs and business management. Much of what I learned in culinary school was helpful at McDonald's, and vice versa. Going to culinary school has played out well in my career.

I was still in culinary school and only nineteen years old when I was promoted to assistant manager, a full-time position. Anywhere from eight to twelve shift managers are under the assistant manager. I did that for about eight months. It was a real lesson in time management.

When I graduated culinary arts school at age twenty, I immediately had a job offer on a cruise ship. I saw it as a way to see the world while making a lot of money. As exciting as the opportunity was, I felt awful about leaving the restaurant family and couldn't help crying when I announced my decision. Everyone was sad.

I had arranged to have a month off before starting on the cruise ship. During that time I learned I was pregnant. My plan to see the world would have to wait.

The owner/operator at the restaurant was glad to have me back, and within two years I was promoted to general manager of the second-highest grossing location of the franchisee's fourteen restaurants. With some sixty people reporting to me and $3.1 million in annual sales, it was overwhelming. I had to learn to take one day at a time.

One of the most important lessons was accepting that everybody couldn't be 100 percent happy all the time. I learned to manage all those people by listening to them, letting them know that I cared about their concerns, and telling them I would try my best for them. I always took time to talk to people in person about their progress, so they would know they were important to me.

Being a successful restaurant manager involves more than people. The business side of managing food costs, sales growth, profit, customer experience, and so on is just as important. I managed that restaurant for four years and was recognized by McDonald's three times as an Outstanding Restaurant Manager. In 2010, I received a Ray Kroc Award, which is given to the top one percent of restaurant managers for achieving operational excellence. I had to go through interviews and a thorough review of every aspect of the business. In our Southern California region, I was one of eight chosen out of 800. It was a big deal.

Now I'm twenty-five and supervisor of four restaurants with about 200 people reporting to me. I'm learning how to empower managers to deal with things I used to. My youth can still be a challenge for people who have been managers for many years. I have to prove to them that I am knowledgeable and mean what I say. I do this by setting an example. For instance, I can't expect people to be friendly if I'm not friendly. If I say we need to improve customer service, I can't expect others to improve it without being good at it myself.

If I need to approach someone about correcting a behavior, I don't do it in front of others. I think this shows respect. When I walk into one of my restaurants, I look around to see if people are smiling and things are moving in the right direction. If I see somebody at the register scowling, I don't go to that person; I go to the manager, who is that person's boss. I first ask him or her to make sure the crew member is okay, and then to give a reminder about being friendly to customers. That way, the boss is aware of what needs to be improved and can address it directly.

I understand that sometimes life happens and people aren't at their best, so I treat the managers the same way. If one is frowning, I ask, "Is everything okay?" If the manager smiles and nods, I say, "You've smiled at me, so make sure you smile for the customers, too."

Someday I'd like to be an owner/operator, but in the meantime I still have a lot of challenges and opportunities with my new position. My director of operations says I'm hard on myself, so I still have a lot more learning and growing to do.

My career so far has been amazing, and my friends and family are proud of how quickly I've become so successful at McDonald's. I look forward to the opportunities ahead.

DID YOU KNOW?

2002: National launch of the Dollar Menu, which offered eight products for one dollar each.

Grand Finale: Two Voices

AUTHOR'S NOTE

Every two years McDonald's hosts a gathering of franchisees and executives from around the world in Orlando, Florida. More than 15,000 people attend. In 2006, the company inaugurated its Voice of McDonald's competition, inviting managers and crew members to compete in an *American Idol* style contest. It culminates with the three finalists performing before the entire crowd in Orlando and a panel of music industry experts as judges. It's a big deal and many of those who get to the semifinals have had opportunities open up for them that they might never have had otherwise. In 2010, there were two contestants selected to be among the twelve semifinalists who had compelling stories. One was the oldest semifinalist and the other the youngest. They both worked for the same owner/operator in Michigan, yet they had never met until they were chosen. Their remarkable stories seemed a perfect way to wrap up what has been an extraordinary journey for me and, I hope, an inspiring read for you.

HIRED 2003

Eddie Davenport

You can pursue a dream at
whatever stage of life you're in.

*I*n 1988 I was diagnosed with a progressive eye disease—a rare form of retinitis pigmentosa—that causes limited vision. By 1993 I had been declared legally blind. I'm not totally blind, but there is a blind spot in the middle of my visual path and my peripheral vision is a bit cloudy. It's not immediately obvious to people who don't know I have a problem.

When I was classified legally blind, my employer of twelve years—a manufacturer of janitorial equipment—asked me to resign. All they said was, "Thanks, but we don't need you anymore." It didn't dawn on me how poorly I was treated until later, when people I mentioned it to reacted with astonishment.

Later that year, my wife, Nora, and I started a children's ministry, visiting churches to do family crusades, singing and performing puppet skits. People told me I had a lot of personality. They were being kind—I just enjoy making people laugh. Doing different voices came easily to me and soon I was working with puppets at a community theater.

In 1994, we went to Michigan for a family crusade. That church needed a children's minister, so we worked there for nine years. The church gave us a place to stay, but my salary was menial, so Nora got a job at McDonald's.

I still loved doing puppetry and working with the kids at the church, but it had been a while and we wanted to move on to something else. Our own children were getting older. After I resigned from the church, I applied for a part-time job at McDonald's. Nora was already there, so I figured I'd give it a try too.

Scott Karns, the owner/operator of the restaurant, had known me for about a year through Nora. The same manager who hired Nora interviewed me. I explained my vision issue. "I can still see enough to do anything your primary maintenance can do. I can't work on anything intricate, like electrical or plumbing, but try me out for a week and see if you want to keep me." After a trial week, they hired me.

I took care of general maintenance—checking the bathrooms, emptying the trash cans, and filtering the cooking oil. The oil got as hot as 350 degrees, but I wore protective equipment so it wasn't that dangerous. I also unloaded trucks. As long as someone else could read the box labels and tell me where to put them, I was fine.

I was so grateful for the chance to work because I couldn't even apply for most jobs. Having a job and earning a living working on a crew and working with a team was a big confidence builder.

The restaurant, in Stockbridge, Michigan, was one of three owned by the Karnses. I worked there for five years, during which time Nora became the restaurant manager. In 2007 she mentioned to me that the company had a singing contest. "I think you should enter it." I had never done anything like that before, but I made a ragtag video of me singing "I've Got You Under My Skin." I had her do a close-up of me singing the song, and then when Nora pulled away to a wide shot, you saw that I was singing to a Big Mac. Evidently, that caught the eyes of the judges and I made it to the semifinals before I got cut. It was disappointing, but I really wasn't ready yet.

Two years later I said, "I think I want to try that again." I had been doing a lot of practicing, so I made a video with my granddaughters of a song called "Misty." I sent it in and again made it to the semifinals. This time I was moved to the next level of competition, and we were told to make another, more professional video that McDonald's would pay for. I thought, This is cool!

We sent the video in and waited and waited, and by December 2009 I figured I had gotten cut. But one morning I came into the restaurant and the whole lobby was full of people, with two local news crews and a camera crew from the corporate office. It was fantastic. Scott announced, "Eddie Davenport, you're going to Orlando!" I became the oldest finalist they'd had in the Voice of McDonald's competition.

After the hoopla died down, they dragged me over to one of Scott's other locations so that I could be there when Fatima Poggi found out she was a finalist too. We were chosen out of 10,451 submissions from around the world. She was the youngest semifinalist ever, so we made a nice pair of bookends.

The trip to Orlando was amazing. McDonald's spared no expense, treating us like royalty. They provided us with the best vocal coaches, and I learned so much and made great friendships. The other finalists are still my friends, even though they're on the other side of the world.

For my performance I chose "Broken Vow" by Josh Groban. It was not my best performance, but I did learn something that I've put into practice. Any time that you have a song that has even one note in it that intimidates you, don't sing the song. Otherwise your only focus when you get out on the stage is going to be that one note. Am I going to hit it? Am I going to make it?

I didn't make it to the top three but people were telling me, "Eddie, you're an inspiration. You have this visual disability, but you didn't let that defeat you. You kept trying." I had no idea that I was having that kind of effect on people.

One of the entertainment professionals involved in the Orlando event told me, "Eddie, you just wear your soul on the outside. You're so genuine." So I wrote a song, which is on my latest CD, titled "Wear Your Soul on the Outside." That was really cool.

I continued with my lessons after that because this whole competition reignited something inside of me—the joy of singing. I've decided to pursue my dream. I never would have done that had I not been involved in the Voice of McDonald's.

After the competition I did a number of appearances at McDonald's events. In December 2011, Nora and I moved to Georgia, and I started going for auditions. I have made two jazz/big band CDs and recorded my first country CD. I had been contemplating writing a children's book and finally wrote it. Now I'm looking for a publisher.

One of the reasons McDonald's liked having me sing at their events is that I'm an example of a person with a disability who became a successful employee. Their support motivated me to inspire others to pursue their dreams, especially those who are older. All the good stuff in life is not just for young people. Just because you hit a certain age, you don't have to quit. You can keep trying and can pursue a dream at any stage of life.

After all, Ray Kroc himself didn't get started with McDonald's until he was in his fifties.

DID YOU KNOW?

2003: Global advertising campaign, "I'm Lovin' It," is launched.

Fatima Poggi

AUTHOR'S NOTE

How is it possible for someone to have a remarkable career one year after they first started working at McDonald's? Fatima Poggi was a young Peruvian-born girl who loved to sing but wasn't sure what she wanted to do with her life. She wanted to buy her first car and that's what brought her to McDonald's. When her owner/operator found out why she was taking so much time off—for singing engagements—he encouraged her to enter the company's international Voice of McDonald's competition. She did, and ended up one of twelve semifinalists out of more than 10,000 entries. Now she has a recording contract and a very bright future as a Latina pop star.

All the people at McDonald's treated me like family and told me if I ever needed anything, they would be there.

When I was ten years old my mother brought me to America from Peru, looking for a better life for me. We settled in Paterson, New Jersey. It was very hard leaving the family and my entire life behind. I remember staying up all night with my mom doing homework and crying because I couldn't understand it. I was used to getting good grades, so not being able to do my homework right or take a test right was very frustrating. But in a matter of months I was speaking English with very few problems.

I did not formally study voice and dance before coming to the States, but I did win my first competition, a school event, when I was four years old in Peru. When I moved to the US, my mom and I tried to look for something that would distract us from feeling lonely. I started taking lessons in Peruvian folk dance called marinera, and I won a lot of competitions around New Jersey, Washington, and Virginia.

After that, we started finding out about Peruvian festivals that happened around Peru's independence day. My mom would knock on doors and talk to the producers of these festivals and say, "Hey, here's this girl who sings." I was twelve years old by then.

The producers would say, "We don't have a budget for it." My mom would tell them that it didn't matter, that she just wanted them to hear me sing. So they gave me the opportunity to do that, and that year I sang in a lot of festivals. The next year, they were the ones who called us.

We've been working on my career ever since. I come from a family of musicians and composers from my dad's and my mom's sides. My mother knew I had it in me.

When I was fourteen, we moved to Michigan because my mom got married and her husband lived there. It was like having to start a new life again, although harder because the Hispanic community was small.

When I was sixteen, I wanted to buy a car. My mom said, "Okay, I'll help you out. But you need to help us out, too." I believe a lot in intuition, and it was very weird that just as I was in the car talking to my mother about starting to work, we stopped at a McDonald's to get breakfast before church. We noticed this huge Now Hiring sign outside.

My mom and stepfather looked at each other and said, "Why not fill out an application while we're here?" It seemed fated to be.

I was told that the manager was in the restaurant and that she could give me the interview right then. It was all very quick and easy. The next day she called and said that I was hired and that I could start working whenever I wanted.

That was in 2009. The first few days that I worked I was very nervous. I started as a front cashier and all the buttons were confusing. After a week, though, I was a pro.

After I was working for a couple of months I started needing time off for singing engagements. One of these was for a voice competition called Cantamare in the Italian community in New York. I have Italian roots on my dad's side, as you can tell from my last name. I won first place, so they sent me to Italy to represent the Italian-American community. So I needed time off to go to Sicily to sing a couple of songs. It was an amazing experience.

I also had an appearance here and there in New Jersey in the Latin festivals. I would be gone for one day during those performances, so I would ask someone else to cover a shift for me, and I would cover for them another day.

One day, Scott Karns, the restaurant owner, called me in during my shift and asked me why I needed so much time off. I thought I was in trouble. I told him that I loved to sing and explained about the competitions, festivals, and performances. He was amazed and interested by everything, and he said, "If you can sing, then sing something for us." In front of all the customers, crew, and managers I sang a song, with everyone staring at me. I sang a Selena song, a Spanish love song called "No Me Queda Mas." It means "Nothing's Left For Me." I was blushing, but at the same time I liked that my friends could see what I could do. Everyone applauded. Then Scott told me about the Voice of McDonald's competition and that he really thought I should enter.

"Well, so many people are auditioning for it," I said. "Maybe I won't even make it."

"You should just try," he said. I was scared, but I had nothing to lose.

I recorded a video singing a Spanish song called "Contigo en la Distancia," that means "With You in the Distance." It's an old love song that was recently covered by Christina Aguilera. My mom and I produced and edited the video together. I thought with so many people competing, nothing would ever come of it.

I sent in the video in August 2009. One day in October I went to work, and Scott said he got a call saying that I made it to the semifinals. I was one of thirty out of the whole world, from over 10,000 entries. I was shocked. I was only sixteen years old.

In order to go to the finalist competition, we had to record another video. But this time they were asking for a more professional video, and McDonald's helped us out with some money for a professional production in a studio. They gave us a list of songs that we could choose from. I decided to sing "Alone" by Heart. I had a feeling that I could move on to the finals.

In December I got the flu and stayed home from school and work one day. The next day I woke up feeling a little better but decided I needed another day to rest and stayed home from school again. When it came time for me to go to work, I decided to call in sick.

"No, you have to go to work today," my mother said.

"But I don't feel well."

"No, you're going to go to work." Her insistence was strange, but I said, "Okay, fine. I'll go to work."

When I got to the restaurant, they had me work the drive-thru window. When you work the drive-thru, you're not only in charge of taking people's money, but you're also in charge of doing the dishes. When I started doing dishes, my shirt got sprinkled with water.

The manager who was in charge that day came back and said, "They're calling you up front." I thought maybe they wanted me on the front cash register. I was a mess because my shirt was all wet, but I started to go and the manager said, "Are you going to go like that?"

"Yeah. Why?"

"No, no, no. Here," and she started cleaning me up and fixing my hair.

Now I could tell something was up. "What are you doing?"

I walked out front and saw all these people standing in front of the counter—my mom and my family and Scott and people I didn't know wearing suits, and there was this huge camera. Scott had a big smile on his face. He said, "You made it to the finals! You're going to the worldwide competition in Orlando." I was now one of twelve.

The competition was the following April at McDonald's biannual worldwide convention, where I would be performing in front of 15,000 people. I started taking voice lessons and doing everything to get ready. My parents and I were flown in a week before the competition. When we got there, we were settled into a really amazing hotel and got first-class treatment. We spent a week with professional coaches and directors. I chose to sing "Note to God" by Charice. I didn't get to the final three, but what happened to me after was almost as good as winning.

After the competition, I got many opportunities with McDonald's. I started recording commercials for their website, and I did a radio commercial for their Hiring Day.

I went back to working in the restaurant until the fall. Sometimes the crew badgered me into singing while I worked. When I turned eighteen and could legally enter into contracts, the opportunities really opened up. I was signed to a recording contract with Artists and Brands agency. My producer is Ira Antelis and one of the partners is Rodney Jerkins, who has produced Michael Jackson, Beyoncé, Whitney Houston, Lady Gaga, and many other awesome artists.

When I left the restaurant for the last time as a crew member, Scott Karns and all the people at McDonald's treated me like family and told me if ever I needed anything, they would be there.

Sometimes I think about how lucky I was to see that Now Hiring sign.

DID YOU KNOW?

2009: The Mac Snack Wrap is introduced.

2010s?

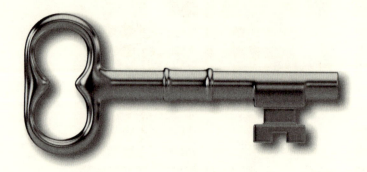

The Golden Opportunity Keys To Success

The following are distilled from all the lessons that the people profiled here mentioned as being important factors in their journeys.

- No task is beneath you, even cleaning a bathroom.
- Teamwork means pitching in without being asked.
- Leadership means stepping up when you are needed.
- Own your mistakes and build on them.
- Take pride in a skill mastered, no matter how basic.
- Take pride in a job well done, no matter how small.
- Roll with the punches, stay focused under pressure.
- Never compromise product or service standards.
- Study the successes of others and learn from them.
- Work hard and smile often.

Learn more at www.GoldenOpportunityBook.com

HIRED 201?

Who's Next?

You've reached the end of the road and I hope you have come to the conclusion that it isn't a dead end.

For me, the completion of this project, a five-year journey, reminds me to ask myself, "What's next?" I don't have an answer yet, but I hope it includes playing a role in debunking the myth of the dictionary definition of a McJob.

Whether or not there is a quick-service restaurant in your future, the next time you patronize any business that employs young people in entry-level jobs, you might remember that the person serving you could just turn out to be the next Jeff Bezos, Jay Leno, or an astronaut, or a corporate executive.

You might ask yourself if the teenager who seems to be fumbling with the keys on the register is just scared because it's her first day and she wants to do a good job because she needs the money. Maybe she just wants her mom and dad to be proud when she brings home her first real paycheck. Maybe the money will buy that bus ticket to New York and a career in show business. Maybe it'll buy groceries for the family.

Maybe it'll just give that young man or woman a first taste of independence that will help build the self-confidence he or she will need to pursue a dream, conquer the world, or just live a satisfying life.

You don't have to be famous or rich to have a remarkable career. You just have to keep asking yourself, "What's next?"